Parallels

ENGLISH GRAMMAR

Brent Davis Reid

Parallels

ENGLISH GRAMMAR

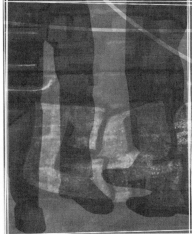
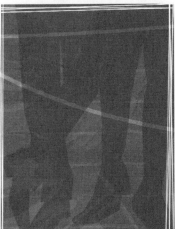

PEARSON
Longman

DISTRIBUTED IN CANADA BY ERPI
5757, RUE CYPIHOT, SAINT-LAURENT (QUÉBEC) H4S 1R3
TELEPHONE: **(514) 334-2690** ext. **232**   FAX: **(514) 334-0448**
infoesl@erpi.com   **w w w . l o n g m a n e s l . c a**

ACKNOWLEDGEMENTS

Many thanks to:

friends and family members for their much needed encouragement;

Sharnee Chait for her insightful comments;

the entire ERPI team for their matchless professionalism (and warm welcome!);

the talented team at Dessine-moi un mouton.

In memory of Sandra Seggie.

Managing editor
Sharnee Chait

Editor
Lucie Turcotte

Copy editor
Padmini Sukumar

Proofreader
My-Trang Nguyen

Production supervisor
Muriel Normand

Cover, book design and page layout
Dessine-moi un mouton

© 2006 Published and distributed by

ÉDITIONS DU RENOUVEAU PÉDAGOGIQUE INC.

Registration of copyright: Bibliothèque et Archives nationales du Québec, 2006
Registration of copyright: Library and Archives Canada, 2006
Printed in Canada

ISBN 2-7613-1729-7

123456789 IO 9876
131729 ABCD 0F10

TABLE OF CONTENTS

What Are Your Thoughts?

A sentence is a word or a group of words that has a stated or implied subject, a verb and expresses a complete thought.

> Go!
> Bob is leaving.

A sentence may be affirmative, negative or interrogative.

> She studies.
> She does not study.
> Does she study?

In this unit, we will examine three types of sentences that people use when writing down their thoughts.

Did You Know?

There are three basic types of sentences:

1. **Simple**
   Mr. Johnson is a teacher.

2. **Compound**
   Kevin is a student, and he works part-time.
   Mary is tired; however, she will finish the work.
   Edith is leaving; she is going home.

3. **Complex**
   Tell Charlie to call me when he gets up.
   Because he works hard, he does well in English.

Simple Sentences

Another term for a simple sentence is an "independent clause."

A simple sentence has only one independent clause, typically comprising one subject and one verb.

Compound Sentences

A compound sentence has two (or more) independent clauses. There are three basic types.

Type	Descriptions	Examples
1	Two (or more) independent clauses linked by a *coordinate conjunction*.	Kent eats well, *and* he exercises.
2	Two (or more) independent clauses linked by an *adverbial conjunction*.	Mary bought a new sound system; *furthermore*, she bought a plasma TV.
3	Two (or more) independent clauses linked by a semicolon.	I walk fast; she walks slowly.

Note: • The coordinate conjunction is preceded by a comma.
　　　　• The adverbial conjunction is preceded by a semicolon and followed by a comma.

There are seven coordinate conjunctions.

Coordinate Conjunctions	Functions	Examples
and	To add	Sally moved to Toronto, *and* she got a job.
nor	To add an idea after a negative statement	He didn't laugh, *nor* did he cry.
but	To contrast	Jennifer got an A, *but* Anne got a B.
for	To introduce a reason	Christopher did well on his test, *for* he worked hard.
yet	To introduce two opposing ideas	I slept well, *yet* I am still tired.
so	To show a result	He worked hard, *so* he made a lot of money.
or	To show an alternative	You can do the dishes, *or* you can take out the trash.

Note: • Nor is followed directly by an auxiliary + subject + simple form of the verb: *She doesn't work, nor **does** she study.*
　　　　• As a coordinate conjunction, *for* means "because."

There are many adverbial conjunctions. Some of the more common are listed below.

Adverbial Conjunctions	Functions	Examples
furthermore moreover	To add	Tina's parents bought her a car; *furthermore*, they paid for her studies.
however nevertheless	To contrast	Todd does well in school; *however*, he is not enjoying his studies.
indeed in fact	To emphasize	Jenny did well on her test; *indeed*, she received a perfect grade.
consequently therefore	To show a result	They arrived late for work every day last week; *consequently*, they were fired.
otherwise	To show an alternative consequence	Arrive at work on time; *otherwise*, you will be fired.
meanwhile	To show simultaneous actions	Susan was rushing about; *meanwhile*, her husband was taking a nap.

Note: Coordinate and adverbial conjunctions can express similar functions: to add, to contrast, to show a result and to show an alternative.

Complex Sentences

A complex sentence has two (or more) clauses, at least one of which is a dependent clause.

A dependent clause begins with a subordinate conjunction (or dependent marker) such as *because*: the idea expressed is incomplete. To complete the idea, an independent clause is required.

<u>*Because she had run five miles,*</u> <u>*Shelly was exhausted.*</u> } complex sentence
      dependent clause   independent clause

Some of the more common subordinate conjunctions are listed below.

Subordinate Conjunctions	Functions	Examples
as / just as	To make a comparison	You will do *as* you are told.
if / unless	To set a condition	*If* it rains, she will stay home.
whether	To introduce a choice	She does not seem to care *whether* she lives or dies.
as long as	To introduce a period of time	He will love her *as long as* he lives.
where / wherever	To introduce a place	He will go *where* she goes.
because	To give a reason	*Because* the students were on strike, classes were cancelled.
although even though	To present opposing ideas	*Although* she likes mathematics, she is not doing well in his course.
since / when	To refer to a point in time	*Since* they got married, they have been fighting like cat and dog.
before / after	To establish a sequence	*Before* they went to class, they had reviewed their notes.
while	To show simultaneous actions	They were in chemistry class *while* their friends were in French class.

Note: Sentences containing relative clauses are also complex sentences. Relative clauses are introduced by relative pronouns such as *who, whom, that, which* and *whose*.
    The student **who ran five miles** was exhausted.
Relative pronouns and clauses will be examined further in Unit 9.

Would You Like to Practise?

Exercise 1

■ **Indicate whether each of the following sentences is a simple, compound or complex sentence. The first one has been done for you.**

Sentences	Sentence Types		
	Simple	Compound	Complex
1. Everybody knows it is wrong to be dishonest; nevertheless, everybody is dishonest from time to time.		*X*	
2. Have you ever done anything wrong?			
3. If a woman stole an apple to feed her son, would the theft be wrong?			
4. If you have never done anything wrong, you have lived an exceptional life.			
5. Lying is sometimes wrong, and it is sometimes right.			
6. Return the stolen goods; otherwise, you will be fired.			
7. She despises him, for he hurt her deeply.			
8. She did not get caught; she did not go to jail.			
9. He has gossiped about his friends and his family.			
10. You will be punished unless you confess.			

Exercise 2

■ **Create compound sentences by correctly matching the independent clauses.**

Independent Clause	Independent Clause
1. Kevin lied to his girlfriend, `g`	a) nor did he visit her.
2. They tried to do their homework, ☐	b) for there is a storm coming.
3. Carl did not call her, ☐	c) yet I still got in trouble.
4. She loves him, ☐	d) or I will call the police.
5. I told the truth, ☐	e) and we cried.
6. Return the money, ☐	f) nor could they forget.
7. We laughed, ☐	g) so she left him.
8. They couldn't forgive, ☐	h) for he loves her.
9. You must leave soon, ☐	i) or you can have happiness.
10. You can have money, ☐	j) but they couldn't understand it.

Exercise 3

■ **Create compound sentences by joining each pair of independent clauses with a coordinate conjunction.**

1. The police didn't catch the robbers. They didn't find the stolen goods.
   The police didn't catch the robbers, nor did they find the stolen goods.

2. He asked her a direct question. She did not answer him.

3. Her father lent her his BMW. She drove to school.

4. She felt guilty. She did not confess.

5. She had a car accident. She was not upset.

6. She wanted to know. She did not ask.

7. The defendant confessed. The judge was lenient.

8. They can forgive. They can forget.

9. They work hard. They want to succeed.

10. We can tell the truth. We can lie.

Exercise 4

- Create compound sentences by correctly matching the independent clauses.

Independent Clause		Independent Clause
1. The teacher caught the student cheating;	_h_	a) nevertheless, no one believed her.
2. Elise is in great shape;	☐	b) moreover, she is a bald-faced liar!
3. Work hard;	☐	c) consequently, she is in good shape.
4. She told the truth;	☐	d) indeed, she is in the best shape of her life!
5. Harriet is a gossip;	☐	e) furthermore, they paid for the honeymoon.
6. George is playing basketball;	☐	f) in fact, she is the best teacher in the school.
7. Sherry is a good teacher;	☐	g) meanwhile, his best friend Steve is in philosophy class.
8. Jane exercises every day;	☐	h) therefore, the student was suspended.
9. Her parents paid for the wedding;	☐	i) however, they don't want to have any of their own.
10. They love children;	☐	j) otherwise, you won't succeed.

Exercise 5

- Create compound sentences by joining each pair of independent clauses with an adverbial conjunction.

1. Dana was found guilty of plagiarism. She was expelled from university.
   Dana was found guilty of plagiarism; consequently, she was expelled from _____
   university. _____

2. Do the assignment in class. You will have to complete the assignment at home.
   _____

3. He stole a car. He went to jail.
   _____

4. Kieran was practising karate. His girlfriend Pam was playing soccer.
   _____

5. She lost her job. She couldn't pay the rent.

_____

6. She told a fib. She felt guilty.

_____

7. There's a terrible snowstorm outside. I will drive to school.

_____

8. They are quite rich. They are multimillionaires.

_____

9. We work hard. We play hard.

_____

10. William worked hard on the team assignment. He did almost all of the work himself.

_____

Exercise 6

■ **Create complex sentences by joining the clauses with a subordinate conjunction.**

1. Christine and Karine met for the first time. They liked each other immediately.
When Christine and Karine met for the first time, they liked each other
immediately.

2. Harry handed in his essay. He had checked his spelling.

_____

3. He doesn't know. He should go to university or get a job.

_____

4. It snows. She will not go.

_____

5. Mr. and Mrs. Jenkins are getting a divorce. One of them had an affair.

_____

6. Richard works hard. He never seems to get ahead.

_____

7. They will love each other. They live.

_____

8. They will get good grades. They will study hard.

_____

9. You were working. They were playing video games.

_____

10. You do all the grammar exercises. You will get a great mark on your next test.

_____

Exercise 7

▬ **Use the following coordinate, adverbial and subordinate conjunctions to write compound and complex sentences of your own.**

1. although: _____

_____

2. for: _____

_____

3. however: _____

_____

4. indeed: _____

_____

5. nor: _____

_____

6. otherwise: _____

_____

7. therefore: _____

_____

8. whether: _____

_____

9. while: _____

_____

10. yet: _____

_____

Exercise 8

■ Fill in the blanks with the following coordinate, adverbial and subordinate conjunctions:

• after	• and	• but	• in fact	• where
• although	• because	• however	• nevertheless	• while

Have you every heard of Edwin Alonzo Boyd and the Boyd gang?

Eddie Boyd was a Canadian bank robber in the late 40s and early 50s; **1.** _____*nevertheless*_____, he is considered by many to be a Canadian folk hero.

Eddie Boyd was handsome; **2.** _____, he bore a striking resemblance to Errol Flynn, a handsome Hollywood film star of the day. **3.** _____ he was strikingly good-looking and charming, Boyd developed a reputation as a "gentlemanly" bank robber; **4.** _____, his exploits were far from gentlemanly.

5. _____ he had committed a series of robberies, Boyd was caught and sent to the infamous Don Jail in Toronto. **6.** _____ he was in jail, Boyd met two other bank robbers: Lennie Jackson and Willie Jackson. Together they hatched a plan, **7.** _____ on November 4, 1951, they escaped from jail. They soon met up with Valent Lesso (a.k.a. Steve Suchan), and the Boyd gang was born.

After committing a string of daring robberies, Willie Jackson was caught and sent back to jail. The remaining three members went into hiding, **8.** _____ they were soon caught as well. Steve Suchan and Lennie Jackson were arrested after a shootout in which Detective Sergeant Ed Tong was killed. Boyd himself was arrested shortly thereafter. All four ended up back in the Don Jail **9.** _____ they had previously been imprisoned. Within six months the gang escaped—again!

10. _____ all four were eventually caught and sent back to prison, only Willie Jackson and Eddie Boyd were ever released from jail: Steve Suchan and Lennie Jackson were hanged for the murder of Ed Tong.

Exercise 9

- On a separate sheet of paper, write a 50- to 75-word paragraph in which you relate an anecdote about getting caught doing something wrong (or catching someone else doing something wrong).

- Use a variety of sentence types: simple, compound and complex.

Exercise 10

- Correct each of the sentences below.
- Rewrite the correct sentence.

1. He copied the ~~answers but~~ he didn't get caught.

   Correction(s): *He copied the answers, but he didn't get caught.*

2. She doesn't lie, nor she does steal.

   Correction(s): _____

3. They must study; otherwise they won't pass.

   Correction(s): _____

4. She does, as her mother says.

   Correction(s): _____

5. Because they plagiarized they didn't learn anything.

   Correction(s): _____

6. He went to jail, where he learned how to be a better criminal.

   Correction(s): _____

7. They cheated on their test, because they hadn't studied.

   Correction(s): _____

8. We can go out for Chinese food or we can go out for Italian food.

   Correction(s): _____

9. I will inform your parents, whether you like it or not.

   Correction(s): _____

10. Before they finally got caught they had robbed three banks.

    Correction(s): _____

Activity 1: Sentence Completion

In this activity, you will practise complex sentences with a partner.

Required
• Sentence Completions Worksheet (below)
• A pen or a pencil
• A dictionary

Instructions
1. Working individually, each partner completes his/her part of the worksheet.

2. Student A reads his/her first sentence completion with Student B.

3. Student B responds to Student A's completion, asking for more information. For example:
   Student A: *If I won a million dollars, I would buy a new car.*
   Student B: *What kind of car would you buy?*

4. Student B reads his/her first sentence completion with Student A.

5. Student A responds to Student B's completion, asking for more information.

6. Repeat steps 2–5 until all sentence completions have been read and responded to.

Suggestion: Exchange sentence completions and repeat the activity—or make up similar sentence completions of your own.

Sentence Completions Worksheet

Student A
1. If I won a million dollars, I would _____

   _____

2. If I could meet any famous deceased person, I would most like to meet

   _____

3. If I could be any famous person I wanted, I would be _____

   _____

4. If I could choose any profession I wanted, I would choose to be _____

   _____

5. If I could be any animal I wanted, I would be _____

   _____

Student B

1. If I could meet any famous living person, I would most like to meet

   _____

2. If I could ask God any question at all, I would ask him/her why _____

   _____

3. If I could be any age at all, I would most like to be _____

   _____

4. If I could trade places with any person at all, I would trade places with

   _____

5. If I were the prime minister of the country, I would _____

   _____

Activity 2: Compound Sentences

In this activity, you will practise compound sentences in teams of three or four.

Required
- 20 sheets of paper, ten for each team
- A pen or a pencil
- A dictionary

Instructions
1. Using a variety of coordinate and adverbial conjunctions, each team writes ten compound sentences, one on each sheet of paper.

2. Team members cut each sheet of paper in two, separating the clauses.

3. Each team "shuffles" the sheets of paper and hands them to the opposing team.

4. Each team must re-create the other team's original sentences.

5. The first team to complete the task wins.

Suggestion: Repeat the activity, this time using subordinate conjunctions to create complex sentences.

Is There Really No Time Like the Present?

"There's no time like the present!"

This expression is often used to warn procrastinators to stop wasting time and "get down to business!"

People often procrastinate when faced with a difficult task–like preparing for a test, writing an essay or studying English grammar! However, once they "get going," they usually find the task wasn't nearly as difficult as they had imagined.

In Unit 2, we're going to study two different present tenses:

1. **The simple present**
2. **The present continuous**

Did You Know?

The Simple Present Tense

The simple present is used to express:

- General or repeated actions
  *She **eats** a big breakfast **on the weekend**.*

- Facts
  *People **eat** breakfast **in the morning**.*

Key Terms:

in the morning, every morning, every afternoon, every day, often, on the weekend, in general, always, often, as a rule …

Let's examine the following conjugation chart.

> **GRAMMAR TIP**
> The third person singular (*he, she, it*) takes an "s" in the affirmative; all other persons (*I, you, we, they*) do not.

Affirmative	Negative	Interrogative
I eat.	I do not eat. (I don't eat.)	Do I eat?
You eat.	You do not eat. (You don't eat.)	Do you eat?
He/She/It eats.	He/She/It does not eat. (He/She/It doesn't eat.)	Does he/she/it eat?
We eat.	We do not eat. (We don't eat.)	Do we eat?
They eat.	They do not eat. (They don't eat.)	Do they eat?

Note: • In the negative and interrogative forms, the auxiliary *does* is used for the third person singular and *do* is used for all other persons.
- In the negative and interrogative forms, only the auxiliary is conjugated.
- In the negative form, the contractions *don't* and *doesn't* are formed by substituting an apostrophe for the letter "o" and contracting two words into one.
- In the interrogative form, the auxiliary precedes the subject.

A yes/no question is a question to which the answer is either yes or no. To transform a yes/no question into an information question, place the question word before the auxiliary:

Does he eat? ➡ **Why** *does he eat?*
Do they eat? ➡ **Where** *do they eat?*

Spelling Hints:
• Add "s" to most verbs in the third person singular.
answer ➡ *answers*

• If the verb ends in "ch," "sh," "s" or "x," add "es."
catch ➡ *catches wash* ➡ *washes*
miss ➡ *misses fix* ➡ *fixes*

• If the verb ends in "y," change the "y" to "i" and add "es."
study ➡ *studies*

Pronunciation of Final "S"

There are three ways to pronounce the final "s":

1. As an /s/ sound: *eats, talks, walks* …
2. As a /z/ sound: *lives, loves, moves* …
3. As an /iz/ sound: *kisses, fizzes, washes* …

Pronounce the final "s" as an /s/ sound when the last sound of the verb is voiceless.

Pronounce the final "s" as a /z/ sound when the last sound of the verb is voiced.

Pronounce the final "s" as an /iz/ sound when the simple form of the verb ends in "s," "z," "sh," "ch," "x," "se," "ge" or "ce."

The Verb *Be*

The verb *be* is conjugated differently from all other verbs.

Take a look at the conjugation chart below.

Affirmative	Negative	Interrogative
I am here. (I'm here.)	I am not here. (I'm not here.)	Am I here?
You are here. (You're here.)	You are not here. (You're not here. You aren't here.)	Are you here?
He/She/It is here. (He's/She's/It's here.)	He/She/It is not here. (He's/She's/It's not here. He/She/It isn't here.)	Is he/she/it here?
We are here. (We're here.)	We are not here. (We're not here. We aren't here.)	Are we here?
They are here. (They're here.)	They are not here. (They're not here. They aren't here.)	Are they here?

Note: • The first person singular (*I*) and the third person singular (*he, she* or *it*) have different conjugations from the other persons: *am* and *is* are used, not *are*. No auxiliary is required.
• In the negative form, contractions can be formed in two different ways for all persons but the first person singular.
• In the interrogative form, the verb precedes the subject.

To transform a yes/no question into an information question, place the question word before the verb:

Is he here? ➡ **Why** *is he here?*

The Present Continuous Tense

The present continuous is used to express:

• Actions occurring now
  *She is eating breakfast **at the moment**.*

• Planned future actions
  *They are eating breakfast **in an hour**.*

Key Terms:
at the moment, in an hour, now, right now, at this very minute, in a couple of hours, tomorrow, next week, next month …

The present continuous is composed of an auxiliary (*be* conjugated in the simple present, see above) and a present participle (verb + "ing"). Examine the following conjugation chart:

Affirmative	Negative	Interrogative
I am eating. (I'm eating.)	I am not eating. (I'm not eating.)	Am I eating?
You are eating. (You're eating.)	You are not eating. (You're not eating. You aren't eating.)	Are you eating?
He/She/It is eating. (He's/She's/It's eating.)	He/She/It is not eating. (He's/She's/It's not eating. He/She/It isn't eating.)	Is he/she/it eating?
We are eating. (We're eating.)	We are not eating. (We're not eating. We aren't eating.)	Are we eating?
They are eating. (They're eating.)	They are not eating. (They're not eating. They aren't eating.)	Are they eating?

Note: • In the negative form, contractions can be formed in two different ways for all persons but the first person singular.
• In the interrogative form, the auxiliary precedes the subject.

PRONUNCIATION TIP
The contractions *we're* rhymes with *her* and *they're* rhymes with *hair*.

To transform a yes/no question into an information question, place the question word before the auxiliary:

Are they eating? ➡ **When** *are they eating?*

GRAMMAR TIP
Non-action verbs (stative verbs) such as *know* cannot be used in the continuous form: ~~I am knowing you.~~ Other non-action verbs include *be, believe, belong, exist, forget, hate, hear, like, love, need, own, possess, prefer, remember, see* and *understand*.

Would You Like to Practise?

Exercise 1

■ Complete the chart below. Watch the spelling. Indicate the pronunciation with a check mark in the correct column.

Base Form	Simple Present, Third Person Singular	Pronunciation of Final "s"		
		/s/	/z/	/iz/
1. go	*goes*		✔	
2. visit				
3. fly				
4. catch				
5. confess				
6. touch				
7. fix				
8. carry				
9. stay				
10. push				

Exercise 2

■ Indicate with a check mark whether each of the verbs is an action or a non-action (stative) verb.

Remember: Non-action verbs cannot be used in the present continuous.

Base Form	Action	Non-Action	Base Form	Action	Non-Action
1. speak	✔		6. belong		
2. smell			7. possess		
3. understand			8. hate		
4. laugh			9. know		
5. smile			10. hear		

Exercise 3

■ Fill in the blanks with the correct form of the verb in the simple present.

■ Underline any key terms. Do not use contractions.

1. Mark (be) _____*is*_____ a huge pop music fan.

2. He (download) _____ music off the Internet almost every day.

3. His favourite artists (be) _____ female vocalists.

4. He (like) _____ Céline Dion, but (not like) _____ Mariah Carey.

5. He always (feel) _____ a little guilty about downloading music.

6. However, he (not have) _____ enough money to pay for all the music.

7. Whenever he (drive) _____ by Céline's Montreal-area mansion, he (not feel) _____ as guilty.

8. It (not look) _____ like she (need) _____ the money.

9. As a rule, fans (download) _____ music, but they (not pay) _____ for it.

10. Mark sometimes (wonder) _____ if they (feel) _____ guilty, too.

Exercise 4

- **Fill in the blanks with the correct form of the verb in the present continuous.**
- **Underline any key terms. Do not use contractions.**

1. <u>Right now</u>, I (try) _____*am trying*_____ to study for tomorrow's English test. My teacher (give) _____ us a quiz on the present tenses.

2. However, I (not concentrate) _____ on the task at hand.

3. I (think) _____ about what I am going to do tonight.

4. In a couple of hours, some friends and I (meet) _____ at a restaurant. We (go) _____ out for a night on the town.

5. First, we (have) _____ supper in a restaurant. We (not eat) _____ at an ordinary restaurant. We (eat) _____ at The Ritz!

6. We (treat) _____ ourselves to an expensive, great meal.

7. Afterwards, we (head) _____ over to Place des Arts to see a musical.

8. An American company (put) _____ on a production of *Mama Mia*.

9. People (say) _____ it's a great show.

10. I (look) _____ forward to tonight's outing—a lot more than tomorrow's English test.

Exercise 5

▬ Write the negative form of each of the sentences below.

▬ Use contractions and rewrite only the subject and verb.

1. Choclair is signing CDs at HMV.
   Negative form: *Choclair isn't signing* _____

2. He is working as a sound technician.
   Negative form: _____

3. Journalist Lindsay Jones lives in British Columbia.
   Negative form: _____

4. Music downloading is stealing.
   Negative form: _____

5. Record companies charge too much money for CDs.
   Negative form: _____

6. Recording artists are losing money.
   Negative form: _____

7. Every day, jobs are lost in the recording industry.
   Negative form: _____

8. Sarah McLachlan is performing in Quebec City.
   Negative form: _____

9. Steve buys a new CD every month.
   Negative form: _____

10. They are taping some music.
    Negative form: _____

Exercise 6

▪ **Transform each of the following affirmative statements into a yes/no question and then into a logical information question with an appropriate answer. (See Appendix A: Common Information Question Words.)**

1. Robert likes classical music because he finds it soothing.

Yes/No Question	*Does Robert like classical music?*
Information Question	*Why does Robert like classical music?*
Answer	*Because he finds it soothing.*

2. Music downloading is legal in Canada.

Yes/No Question	
Information Question	
Answer	

3. The Canadian Record Association is appealing a court ruling because the ruling was against the association.

Yes/No Question	
Information Question	
Answer	

4. Internet Service Providers (ISPs) protect their users' real identities.

Yes/No Question	
Information Question	
Answer	

5. The Recording Industry Association of America is suing hundreds of people for downloading music.

Yes/No Question	
Information Question	
Answer	

6. The record industry makes billions of dollars.

Yes/No Question	
Information Question	
Answer	

7. People in the record industry are losing their jobs.

Yes/No Question	
Information Question	
Answer	

8. Jane's mother likes rapper Choclair.

Yes/No Question	
Information Question	
Answer	

9. Jane and her sister are listening to the Barenaked Ladies.

Yes/No Question	
Information Question	
Answer	

10. She is going to a concert on the weekend.

Yes/No Question	
Information Question	
Answer	

Exercise 7

■ Fill in the blanks with the correct form of the verb in parentheses.

■ Use either the simple present or present continuous. Do not use contractions.

Let me describe myself to you. I (be) ^{1.}_____*am*_____ a young man in my early 40s. (Yes, I said a *young* man!) I am six feet tall and (weigh) ^{2.}_____ ten pounds more than I should! Every day I (promise) ^{3.}_____ myself that I will go on a diet, but I never do. I (have) ^{4.}_____ two dogs that are very spoiled. Their names (be) ^{5.}_____ Bally and Maxwell. Bally (be) ^{6.}_____ a fox terrier, and Maxwell (be) ^{7.}_____ a mutt. Bally (like) ^{8.}_____ to play fetch. Maxwell (not like) ^{9.}_____ to play fetch; he likes to eat … just like me! I (love) ^{10.}_____ to take them for walks. I enjoy people-watching too! Right now, I can see three people in the park: a mother and father and their young daughter. The father (carry) ^{11.}_____ the little girl on his shoulders. The mother

(pick) ^{12.}_____ wildflowers, and the little girl (laugh)
^{13.}_____ out loud. They (have) ^{14.}_____ fun.

Exercise 8

■ On a separate sheet of paper, write a 50- to 75-word paragraph in which you describe yourself.

■ Mention physical traits (height, weight, hair and eye colour, etc.) as well as personality traits (disposition, strong points, weak points, etc.).

■ Mention one activity you like to do, and one you don't like to do. (Use Exercise 7 as an example.)

Exercise 9

■ On a separate sheet of paper, write a 50- to 75-word paragraph in which you describe a picture from a magazine. The picture must be of five or more people who are participating in some kind of activity.

■ Write one sentence about each person, describing his or her actions in detail.

■ If your teacher is collecting the assignment, cut out the picture and submit it with your description.

Exercise 10

■ Correct each of the sentences below.

1. She ~~don't~~ download music.

   Correction(s): *does not or doesn't* _____

2. Why she is going to the concert?

   Correction(s): _____

3. Does he feels guilty about burning CDs?

   Correction(s): _____

4. Does a famous singer really makes a lot of money?

   Correction(s): _____

5. People steals music off the Internet all the time.

   Correction(s): _____

6. Downloading promote new artists and their music.

   Correction(s): _____

7. Music fans is boycotting some of their favourite artists.

   Correction(s): _____

8. Record companies are exploit teenage fans.

Correction(s): _____

9. A CD cost too much.

Correction(s): _____

10. How much you are willing to pay for a CD?

Correction(s): _____

Would You Like to Talk about It?

Activity 1: Family Photos

■ **Work in pairs to practise the simple present and present continuous in this activity.**

Required
• A few personal photos of friends or family members participating in various activities.

Instructions
1. Student A shows a personal photo to Student B, talking about the names of the people in the photo, his/her relationship to them, what they do for a living, etc.
2. Student B asks a few questions about the photo, using the present tenses: Why is she smiling? How old is he? Is she your best friend? Are they singing?
3. Student B shows a personal photo to Student A, talking about the names of the people in the photo, his/her relationship to them, what they do for a living, etc.
4. Student A asks a few questions about the photo, using the present tenses: Why is she happy? How old are they? Is he your cousin?
5. Continue alternating roles until all the photos have been shown.

Activity 2: Magazine Photos

■ **Work in a group of six or more members.**

Required
• Magazine pictures with people in them, one for each participant less one. (If there are five participants, have four pictures; if there are eight participants, have seven pictures, etc.)
• 1 blank sheet of paper.
• File folders, one for each photo and one for the blank sheet of paper. (Note: The folders must all look the same and be opaque.)

Instructions

1. Place each picture in a folder.
2. Place the blank sheet of paper in a folder.
3. Place all folders on a table, mixing them together.
4. Each participant takes a folder.
5. Participants describe what's in their folders. (Note: The person with the blank sheet of paper pretends he/she has a picture and describes his/her "mental picture" in detail.)
6. The participants question one another, trying to determine who has the blank sheet. (Note: The person with the blank sheet of paper "plays along," asking questions to the other participants.)
7. When participants think they know the identity of the person with the blank sheet, they identify the person and all participants open their folders.
8. Repeat the activity as often as desired.

Suggestion: Have a "third person" set the activity up for you. The activity will be more challenging if none of the participants have seen the pictures beforehand.

Is It All in the Past?

"It's all in the past now, isn't it?"

Every once in a while, good friends "fall out": they argue, they stop talking and eventually, they make up! All's forgiven when, "it's all in the past."

While the present moment is really all we ever have (Unit 2), our life stories are largely written in the past.

In Unit 3, we are going to examine two past tenses:

1. The simple past
2. The past continuous

Did You Know?

The Simple Past Tense

The simple past is used to express:

- Completed actions
  *She **ate** a big meal **last night**.*   Past tense of irregular verb *eat*.
  *She **consumed** a big meal **last night**.*   Past tense of regular verb *consume*.

Key Terms:
last night, yesterday, last weekend, last month, last year, five years ago ...

Irregular Verbs

Irregular verbs have irregular past forms: eat ➡ *ate*. The only way to know the form is to memorize it—or refer to an irregular verb chart such as the one found in Appendix B (page 130). Examine the conjugation chart below.

Affirmative	Negative	Interrogative
I ate.	I did not eat. (I didn't eat.)	Did I eat?
You ate.	You did not eat. (You didn't eat.)	Did you eat?
He/She/It ate.	He/She/It did not eat. (He/She/It didn't eat.)	Did he/she/it eat?
We ate.	We did not eat. (We didn't eat.)	Did we eat?
They ate.	They did not eat. (They didn't eat.)	Did they eat?

Note: • In the affirmative form, the verb conjugation is always the same.
• In the negative and interrogative forms, only the auxiliary is conjugated—and it is always the same: *did*.

A yes/no question is created by placing the auxiliary before the subject. To transform a yes/no question into an information question, place the question word before the auxiliary:

***Did** you eat?* ➡ ***What** did you eat?*

The verb *be* is conjugated differently from all other verbs. Take a look at the conjugation chart below.

Affirmative	Negative	Interrogative
I was there.	I was not there. (I wasn't there.)	Was I there?
You were there.	You were not there. (You weren't there.)	Were you there?
He/She/It was there.	He/She/It was not there. (He/She/It wasn't there.)	Was he/she/it there?
We were there.	We were not there. (We weren't there.)	Were we there?
They were there.	They were not there. (They weren't there.)	Were they there?

Note: • *Be* is an "irregular" irregular verb. There are two simple past forms: *was* for the first and third person singular (I, He/She/It) and *were* for all other persons.
• No auxiliary is required.

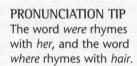

PRONUNCIATION TIP
The word *were* rhymes with *her*, and the word *where* rhymes with *hair*.

A yes/no question is created by placing the verb before the subject. To transform a yes/no question into an information question, place the question word before the verb:

***Was** he there?* ➡ ***Why** was he there?*

GRAMMAR TIP
Some verbs are both regular and irregular.
• The simple past of the verb *burn* can be either *burnt* (irregular) or *burned* (regular).
• The simple past of the verb *learn* can be either *learnt* (irregular) or *learned* (regular). Many verbs have two simple past conjugations.

Regular Verbs

Now let's turn our attention to the regular verbs. Examine the following conjugation chart:

Affirmative	Negative	Interrogative
I consumed.	I did not consume. (I didn't consume.)	Did I consume?
You consumed.	You did not consume. (You didn't consume.)	Did you consume?
He/She/It consumed.	He/She/It did not consume. (He/She/It didn't consume.)	Did he/she/it consume?
We consumed.	We did not consume. (We didn't consume.)	Did we consume?
They consumed.	They did not consume. (They didn't consume.)	Did they consume?

Note: • In the affirmative form, the verb conjugation is always the same (ending with "ed").
• In the negative and interrogative forms, only the auxiliary is conjugated—and it is always the same: *did*.

Spelling Hints:
- Add "ed" to form the simple past of most regular verbs:
  visit ➡ *visited*

- Some verbs ending with a "consonant-vowel-consonant" structure require that you double the last consonant before adding "ed":
  jog ➡ *jogged*

- If the regular verb ends in "y," change the "y" to "i" before adding "ed":
  study ➡ *studied*

- If the regular verb ends in "e," simply add a "d":
  place ➡ *placed*

A yes/no question is created by placing the auxiliary before the subject. To transform a yes/no question into an information question, place the question word before the auxiliary:

Did *you consume?* ➡ **What** *did you consume?*

Pronunciation of "ed"

While the endings of regular verbs are quite regular ("ed"), the pronunciation of these endings is not. There are three ways to pronounce the final "ed" endings of regular verbs:

1. As a /t/ sound: *walked, talked, stopped ...*
2. As a /d/ sound: *planned, exercised, moved ...*
3. As an /id/ sound: *downloaded, landed, planted ...*

PRONUNCIATION TIP
A sound is "voiced" if your vocal cords vibrate when you make the sound—it is "voiceless" if your vocal cords don't vibrate when you make the sound.

Pronounce the final "ed" endings of regular verbs as /t/ sound when the last sound of the verb is voiceless.

Pronounce the final "ed" endings of regular verbs as /d/ sound when the last sound of the verb is voiced.

Pronounce the final "ed" endings of regular verbs as an /id/ sound when the last letters of the verb are "t," "te," "d" or "de."

The Past Continuous Tense

The past continuous is used to express:

GRAMMAR TIP
The past continuous is sometimes called the past progressive. Think about the terms *continuous* or *progressive* to remind yourself to use this tense for ongoing actions only.

- Actions in progress at a specific time in the past
  *She was eating her breakfast **at 8 a.m.***

- Interrupted actions
  *She was eating her breakfast **when** the fire alarm rang.*

- Simultaneous actions
  ***While** she was eating her breakfast, he was making the lunches.*

- Background actions
  *The sun was **shining**, and the birds were **chirping**.*

Key Terms:

at 8 a.m., when, while, at noon, at midnight, at the same time as …

The past continuous is composed of an auxiliary (*be* conjugated in the simple past, see above) and a present participle (verb + "ing"). Examine the following conjugation chart:

Affirmative	Negative	Interrogative
I was eating.	I was not eating. (I wasn't eating.)	Was I eating?
You were eating.	You were not eating. (You weren't eating.)	Were you eating?
He/She/It was eating.	He/She/It was not eating. (He/She/It wasn't eating.)	Was he/she/it eating?
We were eating.	We were not eating. (We weren't eating.)	Were we eating?
They were eating.	They were not eating. (They weren't eating.)	Were they eating?

Note: The present participle is always the same—but remember that the verb *be* has two irregular forms: *was* and *were*.

A yes/no question is created by placing the auxiliary before the subject. To transform a yes/no question into an information question, place the question word before the auxiliary:

Was *he eating?* ➡ **Why** *was he eating?*

> GRAMMAR TIP
> Don't use the past continuous to express past habits, use the simple past instead:
> *jogged*
> *When I was a teenager, I ~~was jogging~~ every day.*

 Would You Like to Practise?

Exercise 1

■ **Test your knowledge of irregular verbs by completing the chart below with the missing simple past forms. (See Appendix B for those you don't know.)**

Irregular Verb	Simple Past	Irregular Verb	Simple Past
1. be	*was, were*	6. drive	
2. begin		7. feel	
3. bring		8. get	
4. buy		9. give	
5. drink		10. leave	

Irregular Verb	Simple Past	Irregular Verb	Simple Past
11. make		16. sit	
12. read		17. sleep	
13. run		18. swim	
14. say		19. take	
15. sing		20. write	

Exercise 2

■ Indicate the correct pronunciation of the final "ed" endings for each of the regular verbs below with a check mark in the appropriate column.

Simple Past Form of Regular Verbs	/t/	/d/	/id/	Simple Past Form of Regular Verbs	/t/	/d/	/id/
1. accepted			✔	11. escaped			
2. announced				12. excited			
3. baked				13. faced			
4. breathed				14. guessed			
5. calculated				15. harmed			
6. called				16. missed			
7. damaged				17. named			
8. danced				18. phoned			
9. depended				19. talked			
10. emptied				20. supported			

Exercise 3

■ Write each of the regular verbs below in the simple past. Watch the spelling.

Base Form	Simple Past	Base Form	Simple Present
1. balance	*balanced*	6. plan	
2. dress		7. educate	
3. agree		8. marry	
4. identify		9. sob	
5. jog		10. kiss	

Exercise 4

- Fill in the blanks with the correct form of the verb in parentheses.
- Use the simple past. Do not use contractions.
- In each sentence, underline any key terms. The first one has been done for you.

(Note: Sentences are in both the affirmative and interrogative forms.)

1. <u>In 1996</u>, the world's first cloned mammal (be) _____*was*_____ born.

2. The first cloned mammal was a sheep (name) _____ Dolly.

3. (Know) _____ you _____ that scientists (call) _____ her Dolly after Dolly Parton because the sheep was cloned from a mammary cell?

4. Dolly (suffer) _____ from premature ageing.

5. Scientists (speculate) _____ that Dolly (age) _____ faster than she should have because she was cloned from a 6-year-old ewe.

6. At the age of five, Dolly (develop) _____ arthritis.

7. At the age of six, scientists (put) _____ Dolly down.

8. She (have) _____ a lung infection.

9. At the time of Dolly's birth, there (be) _____ millions of sheep in Scotland. (Note: "Sheep" is the subject of this sentence.)

10. Many (see) _____ Dolly's birth as unnecessary at best and unethical at worst.

> **GRAMMAR TIP**
> When using the structure "there + *be*," remember that the subject follows *be*.
> ***There was*** one cell. (*Cell* is the subject.)
> ***There were*** many cells. (*Cells* is the subject.)

Exercise 5

- Fill in the blanks with the correct form of the verb in parentheses.
- Use the past continuous. Do not use contractions.
- In each sentence, underline any key terms.

(Note: Sentences are in both the affirmative and interrogative forms.)

Conversation 1

1. When (think) _____*were*_____ you _____*thinking*_____ of leaving for the UK?

2. I (think) _____ of leaving today.

3. My wife and I (plan) _____ on staying in London.

4. The last time we were there, the weather was great—right up until the day we left. As our plane (take) _____ off, it started to rain.

5. We (hope) _____ you could join us this time.

Conversation 2

6. Do you remember what you (do) _____ when you heard about the terrorist attack on New York City?

7. I (live) _____ in St. Sauveur, and I (sit) _____ by the pool.

8. My father told me the news. At first, I thought he (joke) _____.

9. Unfortunately, he (tell) _____ the truth.

10. Thousands of people (die) _____ as the world watched on television.

Exercise 6

- Write the negative form of each of the sentences below.
- Use contractions and rewrite only the subject and the verb.

1. My father grew up in a big family.
   Negative form: *My father didn't grow up* _____

2. He had five brothers and six sisters.
   Negative form: _____

3. His brothers fought all the time.
   Negative form: _____

4. His sisters teased him a lot.
   Negative form: _____

5. He left home on his 18ᵗʰ birthday to get away from them.
   Negative form: _____

6. The other day, I saw him looking at family pictures.

   Negative form: _____

7. He was reminiscing about his younger days.

   Negative form: _____

8. He was smiling as he was looking at the album.

   Negative form: _____

9. He confessed to missing the fighting and the teasing.

   Negative form: _____

10. His confession surprised me.

    Negative form: _____

Exercise 7

■ Transform each of the following affirmative statements into a yes/no question and then into a logical information question with an appropriate answer. (See Appendix A: Common Information Question Words.)

1. The Raelians claimed they had cloned a human.

Yes/No Question	*Did the Raelians claim that they had cloned a human?*
Information Question	*What did the Raelians claim?*
Answer	*That they had cloned a human.*

2. David Suzuki criticized the Raelians.

Yes/No Question	
Information Question	
Answer	

3. He said that human cloning is immoral because it is dangerous.

Yes/No Question	
Information Question	
Answer	

4. Researchers were working in the lab.

Yes/No Question	
Information Question	
Answer	

5. Researchers noticed that cloned animals aged prematurely.

Yes/No Question	
Information Question	
Answer	

6. The cloned mice were suffering from abnormalities.

Yes/No Question	
Information Question	
Answer	

7. Scientists were excited because they had made a breakthrough.

Yes/No Question	
Information Question	
Answer	

8. Jonathan Colvin wanted to clone himself because he wanted a second chance at life.

Yes/No Question	
Information Question	
Answer	

9. He was hoping that cloning wouldn't be made illegal in Canada.

Yes/No Question	
Information Question	
Answer	

10. Reproductive human cloning was criminalized in Canada in 2004.

Yes/No Question	
Information Question	
Answer	

Exercise 8

- Fill in the blanks with the correct form of the verb in parentheses.
- Use either the simple past or past continuous. Do not use contractions.

When I 1._____*was*_____ (be) in university, I 2._____ (not have) much money. To pay my tuition, I had to work part-time in a restaurant.

It _____ ³· (not be) easy, but I somehow _____ ⁴· (manage) to make money and study all at the same time.

Late one evening, I _____ ⁵· (close) up the restaurant when a hooded man _____ ⁶· (walk) in the front door. Without saying a word, he _____ ⁷· (point) a gun at me and _____ ⁸· (tell) me to empty the cash register. I _____ ⁹· (try) to dissuade him but soon _____ ¹⁰· (realize) he _____ ¹¹· (be) very serious. Without another moment's hesitation, I _____ ¹²· (go) to the cash register, _____ ¹³· (open) the drawer and _____ ¹⁴· (empty) its contents on the counter: about a thousand dollars in cash and some credit card slips.

The thief _____ ¹⁵· (pick) up the cash and _____ ¹⁶· (start) towards the door. As he _____ ¹⁷· (walk) out, he _____ ¹⁸· (trip) over his shoelace and _____ ¹⁹· (hit) his head on a table. I couldn't believe my eyes: he had knocked himself out! I immediately _____ ²⁰· (dial) 9-1-1, and the police officers _____ ²¹· (arrive) just as the thief _____ ²²· slowly _____ ²³· (regain) consciousness. He _____ ²⁴· (open) his eyes just as one of the officers _____ ²⁵· (handcuff) him.

As the officers _____ ²⁶· (lead) the thief towards the front door, I _____ ²⁷· (collect) the money, _____ ²⁸· (smile) and _____ ²⁹· (thank) the thief for his generous "trip."

PRONUNCIATION TIP
The last three verbs used in the story are regular verbs. All three have different final "ed" pronunciations. Do you know how to correctly pronounce all three?

Exercise 9

- Write a 50- to 75-word paragraph in which you describe a funny event in your life.
- Set up the background to the story and describe what happened.
- In your description, use both the simple past and past continuous.

Exercise 10

- Correct each of the sentences below.

1. Researchers ~~were wanting~~ to clone a human.
   Correction(s): *wanted* _____

2. The Raelians cloned a human?
   Correction(s): _____

3. Dolly die young.

Correction(s): _____

4. Many animals was cloned in 2004.

Correction(s): _____

5. Did they really cloned a human?

Correction(s): _____

6. Where were they work?

Correction(s): _____

7. Why scientists were cloning mammals?

Correction(s): _____

8. Did all the researchers came to the same conclusion?

Correction(s): _____

9. After working in the lab all day, the technician slept soundly.

Correction(s): _____

10. Why did the *Human Reproduction Act* became law?

Correction(s): _____

Would You Like to Talk about It?

Activity 1: Be Nosy!

Have you ever heard the expression "don't be nosy"? If someone tells you not to be nosy, he (or she) is telling you to mind your own business. In this activity, don't mind your own business: be nosy! Find out all you can about your partner using the simple past and past continuous tenses.

Required
- Questionnaire (below)
- A lot of nerve!

Instructions
1. Read through the questionnaire.
2. Student A begins, asking a question to Student B.
3. If Student B wants to answer the question, he/she does; if not, he/she says, "veto!"

4. Student B continues, asking a question to Student A.
5. If Student A wants to answer the question, he/she does; if not, he/she says, "veto!"
6. Continue until all the questions have been asked—or vetoed!

Suggestion: Ask your partner additional questions based on his/her answers. Be as nosy as you can!

Questionnaire

Student A
1. How old were you when you had your first kiss?
2. Where were you living when you were a child?
3. What were you doing yesterday at 8:00 in the morning?
4. Who was your first boy/girlfriend?
5. How much money did you earn last year?
6. Were you a "good" kid?
7. When you were in primary school, did you ever cheat on a test?
8. What was your last argument about?
9. Did you ever run away from home when you were a young child?
10. What was the funniest thing that happened to you last year?

Student B
1. What were you doing last night at midnight?
2. Who gave you your first kiss?
3. How old were you when you got your first paycheck?
4. What is the silliest thing you did last year?
5. When you were a child, did you ever skip school?
6. How much money did you spend last week?
7. When you were young, did you ever take money from your mother's purse?
8. What was the best gift you got as a child?
9. Did you ever lie to your last boy/girlfriend?
10. What were you doing just before this activity?

Activity 2: Round Robin

A "round robin" is a tournament in which each player is in competition with all other players. In this small group activity, the more players you have, the more challenging the activity.

No materials are required.

Part A
Instructions
1. All players sit in a circle.
2. The first player begins by saying, "Last week was a busy week. I did my English homework."
3. The second player continues by repeating what the first player said, adding another busy activity.
4. The third player continues by repeating what the second player said, adding yet another busy activity.
5. The game continues until only one player is left who can repeat everything that was said: this player is the winner.

Part B

Instructions

1. All players remain in a circle.
2. The winner of Part A of this activity begins the game, this time by saying, "While we were playing this game, my teacher was marking exams."
3. The second player continues by repeating what the first player said, adding another activity.
4. The third player continues by repeating what the second player said, adding yet another busy activity.
5. The game continues until only one player is left who can repeat everything that was said.

Is It Past or Present?

If *you've ever studied* English formally, you've surely come across the present perfect tense. In fact, the sentence *you have just read* is written in this tense, as is the first part of this sentence!

The present perfect is a mixed tense: it is a past tense with a strong connection to the present.

In Unit 4, we are going to examine the present perfect, and compare this tense to the simple past tense studied in Unit 3.

Did You Know?

The present perfect is used to express:

- Actions occurring at an indefinite time in the past
  She has eaten at that restaurant.
  (We don't know *when* she ate there; we just know that she has eaten there.)

- Actions occurring in an incomplete period of time
  I have done my homework **today**.
  (*Today* is not finished.)

- Incomplete actions (or actions beginning in the past and continuing in the present
  They have been in that restaurant **for** *two hours (or* **since** *8:00 o'clock).*
  (They arrived at the restaurant two hours ago, and they are still there now.)

- Recent actions
  They have **just** *finished eating.*
  (A recent action is a past action close in time to the present moment.)

Key Terms:
today, for, since, just, ever, never, yet, this week, this year, recently …

The present perfect is formed by conjugating *have* in the simple present tense and adding the past participle. The past participle of regular verbs is the same as the simple past form: *walk* ➡ *walked* ➡ *walked*. The past participle of irregular verbs varies (see Appendix B): *eat* ➡ *ate* ➡ *eaten*. Examine the conjugation chart on page 38.

Affirmative	Negative	Interrogative
I have eaten. (I've eaten.)	I have not eaten. (I've not eaten. I haven't eaten.)	Have I eaten?
You have eaten. (You've eaten.)	You have not eaten. (You've not eaten. You haven't eaten.)	Have you eaten?
He/She/It has eaten. (He's/She's/It's eaten.)	He/She/It has not eaten. (He's/She's/It's not eaten. He/She/It hasn't eaten.	Has he/she/it eaten?
We have eaten. (We've eaten.)	We have not eaten. (We've not eaten. We haven't eaten.)	Have we eaten?
They have eaten. (They've eaten.)	They have not eaten. (They've not eaten. They haven't eaten.)	Have they eaten?

Note: • The auxiliary *has* is used for the third person singular and *have* for all other persons.
• In the negative form, contractions can be formed in two different ways.
• In the interrogative form, the auxiliary precedes the subject.

To transform a yes/no question into an information question, place the question word before the auxiliary:

Have you eaten? ➡ **What** *have you eaten?*

Questions with Ever and Yet

Compare the following two questions and answers:

1. *Has Karen **ever** eaten at that restaurant?*
➡ *Yes, Karen has eaten at that restaurant.*
➡ *No, Karen has **never** eaten at that restaurant.*

2. *Has Karen eaten at that restaurant **yet**?*
➡ *Yes, Karen has eaten at that restaurant.*
➡ *No, Karen has not eaten at that restaurant **yet**.*

In the first question, the speaker does not know whether Karen has eaten at the restaurant.

In the second question, the speaker does not know whether Karen has eaten at the restaurant—but thinks she will eat there one day.

GRAMMAR TIP
• The adverb *yet* is placed at the end of interrogative and negative sentences.
• *Ever* is placed before the past participle in interrogative sentences.
• *Never* is placed before the past participle in negative sentences.

Comparing the Simple Past and the Present Perfect

Examine the following two sentences:

Simple Past: *I **did** my homework this morning.*
Present Perfect: *I **have done** my homework this morning.*

Both of these sentences are correct—in the right contexts! The first sentence is correct *if it is no longer morning,* while the second sentence is correct *if it is still morning.*

Sometimes, students have difficulty knowing whether to use the simple past or the present perfect.

When unsure which tense to use, ask yourself the following questions:

1. Do I know when the action occurred?
2. Is the period of time in which the action is occurring finished?
3. Is the action finished?
4. Is the action in the distant past?

If the answer to any of these questions is "yes," use the simple past; otherwise, use the present perfect.

Would You Like to *Practise?*

Exercise 1

■ Test your knowledge of the past participles of irregular verbs by completing the chart below. (See Appendix B for those you don't know.)

Irregular Verb	Past Participle	Irregular Verb	Past Participle
1. leave	*left*	11. mean	
2. bend		12. ride	
3. bet		13. ring	
4. catch		14. sell	
5. draw		15. show	
6. fall		16. speak	
7. fly		17. teach	
8. go		18. tell	
9. grow		19. think	
10. lend		20. wear	

Exercise 2

■ **For each of the statements below, underline any key terms and highlight the reason why the present perfect is being used.**

1. <u>In the last twenty years</u>, gay and lesbian activists have won several key court cases.
   Reason: indefinite time; incomplete period of time; incomplete action; recent action

2. The definition of marriage has recently been broadened to include same-sex couples.
   Reason: indefinite time; incomplete period of time; incomplete action; recent action

3. Adam and Steve have been married for ten months.
   Reason: indefinite time; incomplete period of time; incomplete action; recent action

4. They have recently moved into a new house.
   Reason: indefinite time; incomplete period of time; incomplete action; recent action

5. They have adopted twins.
   Reason: indefinite time; incomplete period of time; incomplete action; recent action

6. Their best friends Charles and Brian have never thought about getting married.
   Reason: indefinite time; incomplete period of time; incomplete action; recent action

7. Have Adam's parents sent gifts for the children yet?
   Reason: indefinite time; incomplete period of time; incomplete action; recent action

8. Adam's parents have sent no gifts.
   Reason: indefinite time; incomplete period of time; incomplete action; recent action

9. This year, they have married, bought a house and adopted a child.
   Reason: indefinite time; incomplete period of time; incomplete action; recent action

10. Same sex marriage has been legal since 2005.
    Reason: indefinite time; incomplete period of time; incomplete action; recent action

Exercise 3

■ Fill in the blanks with either *for* or *since*.

Remember: *for* is used with periods of time and *since* is used with points in time.

1. Diane and Caroline have been married _____*for*_____ two months.

2. Diane and Caroline have been married _____ July 20.

3. They have lived at the same address _____ fifteen years.

4. Canadian politicians have fought about same-sex marriage _____ years.

5. Canadians have been divided on the issue of same-sex marriage _____ a long time.

6. Gay and lesbian activists have lobbied the government _____ the mid-1960s.

7. Many Gays and Lesbians have lived in legally recognized common-law relationships _____ 2000.

8. Many have criticized the government _____ Parliament legalized same-sex marriage.

9. Some provincial governments have allowed Gays and Lesbians to adopt children _____ several years now.

10. _____ when has the prime minister been a supporter of gay and lesbian rights?

Exercise 4

■ Fill in the blanks with the correct form of the verb in parentheses.

■ Use the present perfect and do not use contractions.

1. Lisa Fitterman (write) _____*has written*_____ about same-sex adoption.

2. Surrogates (provide) _____ many same-sex couples with children.

3. Some single gay men (decide) _____ to raise children.

4. Most gay men (not opt) _____ to have children.

5. In recent years, primetime TV (portray) _____ positive images of gay and lesbian couples.

6. Homophobia (be) _____ always _____ a part of Canadian society.

7. (experience) _____ most Gays and Lesbians _____ discrimination?

8. Why (act) _____ the government finally _____ on this issue?

9. (read) _____ you _____ the article about same-sex adoption?

10. Unfortunately, I (not have) _____ the time.

Exercise 5

- Fill in the blanks with the correct form of the verb in parentheses.
- Use the present perfect and the simple past.
- Do not use contractions.

Conversation 1

1. Isabella: Where (be) _____*have*_____ you _____*been*_____ ?

2. Dale: I (be) _____ on vacation with Darcy and the kids.

3. Isabella: Where (go) _____ you _____ ?

4. Dale: We (go) _____ to Disneyland.

5. Isabella: How (be) _____ the weather?

Conversation 2

1. Sue: (see) _____ you _____ Hayley and Alex's baby girl?

2. Jane: Yes I (see) _____ her yesterday, sleeping in her crib.

3. Sue: (look) _____ Hayley and Alex _____ tired?

4. Jane: Yes, they (tell) _____ me that they hadn't slept very much.

5. Sue: Well they (have) _____ years to sleep before they (adopt) _____ her. They had better get used to those middle-of-the-night wake-up calls!

Exercise 6

■ **Answer each of the questions in the affirmative and negative forms.**

■ **Use contractions whenever possible.**

■ **For questions with *ever* and *yet*, review the model answers on page 38 before responding.**

1. Have you met the new neighbours from Peru?

   Yes, *I've met the new neighbours from Peru.*

   No, *I haven't (I've not) met the new neighbours from Peru.*

2. Have they ever experienced a Canadian winter?

   Yes, _____

   No, _____

3. Has all their furniture arrived?

   Yes, _____

   No, _____

4. Have they redecorated the house yet?

   Yes, _____

   No, _____

5. Has the neighbourhood association welcomed them?

   Yes, _____

   No, _____

6. Have you invited them over for a meal?

   Yes, _____

   No, _____

7. Have your children played with their children?

   Yes, _____

   No, _____

8. Have their children started to learn French?

   Yes, _____

   No, _____

9. Have the parents enrolled their children in school?

   Yes, _____

   No, _____

10. Has your daughter offered to baby-sit for them?

    Yes, _____

    No, _____

Exercise 7

■ Transform each of the following affirmative statements into a yes/no question and then into a logical information question with an appropriate answer. (See Appendix A: Common Information Question Words.)

1. Pat and Leslie have been married for 12 years.

Yes/No Question	*Are Pat and Leslie married?*
Information Question	*How long have Pat and Leslie been married?*
Answer	*For 12 years.*

2. They have recently bought a big house in the country.

Yes/No Question	
Information Question	
Answer	

3. Pat has quit her job because she wants to stay home.

Yes/No Question	
Information Question	
Answer	

4. Pat and Leslie have decided to adopt two children.

Yes/No Question	
Information Question	
Answer	

5. The couple has gone to China to adopt twin girls.

Yes/No Question	
Information Question	
Answer	

6. The trip to China has cost about $20,000.

Yes/No Question	
Information Question	
Answer	

7. They have met people from the adoption agency.

Yes/No Question	
Information Question	
Answer	

8. They have signed the necessary papers.

Yes/No Question	
Information Question	
Answer	

9. They have made a big change in their lives.

Yes/No Question	
Information Question	
Answer	

10. Pat and Leslie have filled their country house *and* their hearts!

Yes/No Question	
Information Question	
Answer	

Exercise 8

■ Fill in the blanks with the correct form of the verb in parentheses.

■ Use the simple past, the past progressive or the present perfect.

■ Do not use contractions.

(attend) 1. _____*Have*_____ I ever 2. _____*attended*_____ a gay wedding?

Yes, I (be) 3. _____ to a gay wedding.

It (be) 4. _____ in the mid 1980s. I (be) 5. _____ in university at the time and a friend (invite) 6. _____ me over for a drink. While we (have) 7. _____ our drinks, someone (come) 8. _____ and (knock) 9. _____ on the door. It (be) 10. _____ the neighbour. He (have) 11. _____ a party next door, and he (ask) 12. _____ us if we (want) 13. _____ to drop by. He (seem) 14. _____ like a nice guy, so we (agree) 15. _____ .

When we (arrive) _____ 16. , we (be) _____ 17. surprised to see a small group of people in formal attire and a woman dressed as a priest. When we (ask) _____ 18. why she was dressed that way, she (tell) _____ 19. us she had just married the neighbour—and his boyfriend. I (think) _____ 20. she was kidding at first, but I soon (realize) _____ 21. she (be) _____ 22. quite serious.

At first, the idea of two men marrying (seem) _____ 23. odd. After a while, it (not seem) _____ 24. so odd! I soon (relax) _____ 25. and (join) _____ 26. in the celebration.

Since then, I (think) _____ 27. often _____ 28. about that wedding—and my initial reaction to it. I (make) _____ 29. a con-certed effort to keep an open mind when faced with new and "different" situ-ations. It (not be) _____ 30. always _____ 31. easy. But with the years, it (get) _____ 32. easier.

Contrary to what some people say, you *can* teach an old dog new tricks!

Exercise 9

■ Write a 50- to 75-word paragraph about the person who has had the greatest influ-ence on your life.

■ Name the person and explain how this person has influenced you. (What has the per-son taught you? Given you? Shown you? etc.)

■ Begin your paragraph with:
Person's name has had the greatest influence on my life because …

■ Use both the simple past and present perfect tenses.

Exercise 10

■ Correct each of the sentences below.

1. They have ~~adopt~~ their first child.
   Correction(s): *adopted* _____

2. The Church has not recognized yet same-sex marriage.
   Correction(s): _____

3. Friends and family has been very supportive.
   Correction(s): _____

4. Where they have gone?
   Correction(s): _____

5. Brian has ever wanted to own a house.

    Correction(s): _____

6. The baby has cried since about an hour.

    Correction(s): _____

7. Same-sex marriage is legal since 2005.

    Correction(s): _____

8. This week, I did many things.

    Correction(s): _____

9. The adoption of Canada's Civil Marriage Act has shook some Canadians.

    Correction(s): _____

10. They have'nt done anything productive today.

    Correction(s): _____

Would You Like to Talk about It?

Activity 1: Our Past

In this activity, you will have a chance to learn about your partner's past—and the people he or she has encountered.

Required
• Questionnaire (on page 48)
• About ten minutes of your time!

Instructions
1. Read through the questionnaire.
2. Student A begins, asking a "what is" question to Student B.
3. Student B answers the question, beginning in the present perfect and continuing in the simple past.
4. Student B continues, asking a "who is" question to Student A.
5. Student A answers the question, beginning in the present perfect and continuing in the simple past.

> **Example:**
> • Student A: ***What is*** *the worst movie you have ever seen?*
> • Student B: *The worst movie I **have ever seen** is Joe Versus The Volcano.* (present perfect) *I **saw** this movie a long time ago.* (simple past) *I **went** with …etc.*
> • Student B: ***Who is*** *the nicest person you have ever met?*
> • Student A: *The nicest person I **have ever met** is my aunt.* (present perfect) *Just the other day, she **dropped by** with a small gift.* (simple past) *She **gave** me…etc.*

6. Repeat steps 2–5 until all the questions have been asked and answered.

Suggestion: Exchange questions and repeat the activity—or make up similar questions of your own.

Questionnaire

Student A
What is the ...
1. best thing you have ever been given?
2. funniest thing you have ever seen?
3. most interesting experience you have ever had?
4. most beautiful place you have ever visited?
5. most adventurous thing you have ever done?

Student B
Who is the ...
1. most beautiful person you have ever seen?
2. funniest comedian you have ever heard?
3. most successful person you have ever known?
4. strangest person you have ever encountered?
5. most famous person you have ever met?

Activity 2: Truth

In this activity, you will learn about what people have—and have not—done. Work in groups of four to six people.

Required
- 10 pennies for each group member
- Trust!

Instructions
1. Members sit around a table.
2. Each member has ten pennies.
3. The person whose last name is closest to the letter A begins; we'll call this person PLAYER 1.
4. PLAYER 1 tells the group something he/she has *truly* never done, but believes most of the other members have already done. For example, "I have never drunk a glass of beer."
5. Any member who has already drunk a glass of beer must give a penny to PLAYER 1. If another member has also never drunk a glass a beer, PLAYER 1 must give a penny to that person.
6. The turn then passes to the person seated to the right of PLAYER 1.
7. Repeat steps four and five until one of the players loses all of his/her pennies. At this moment, the player with the most pennies is the winner.

Suggestion: Repeat this activity with members talking about things they *have* done but believe others *haven't*; for example, "I have been to Paris."

Note: You may only talk about activities that *everyone* in the group could reasonably be expected to have done. The statement "I have worn a dress" would be unfair to the men in the group in the same way that the statement "I have grown a beard" would be unfair to the women in the group!

UNIT 5 — What Will the Future Be?

None of us can know for certain what the future holds; however, we *can* express our opinions about the future and try to influence its course.

In Unit 2, you saw that the present continuous can be used to express future plans.

*Next year, I **am attending** university.*

In this unit, we are going to examine two other ways of expressing the future:

1. will
2. be going to

Did You **Know?**

Both *will* and *be going to* can be used to express:

- Opinions about the future
  *I hope she will drop by **today**.*
  *I hope she is going to drop by **today**.*

- Predictions
  *I predict it will rain **tomorrow**.*
  *I predict it is going to rain **tomorrow**.*

In most situations, *will* and *be going to* are interchangeable when used to express opinions about the future or make predictions.

Exception: When the predicted action is imminent (about to happen), the *be going to* form is used.

                                    is going to
Look at those dark clouds! It ~~will rain~~ rain any second.

However, in some situations, only *will* can be used; in others, only the *be going to* form can be used.

Will

In addition to expressing opinions about the future and making predictions, *will* is used to express:

- Willingness
  (phone is ringing)
  Bob: *Steve, **will** you **answer** the phone?*
  Steve: *Sure, **I'll get** it.*

- Promises
*I promise I **will** never **leave** you.*

Key Terms
today, tomorrow, promise, next month, next week, next weekend, next year, soon, tonight ...

Let's examine the conjugation chart below.

Affirmative	Negative	Interrogative
I will eat. (I'll eat.)	I will not eat. (I'll not eat. I won't eat.)	Will I eat?
You will eat. (You'll eat.)	You will not eat. (You'll not eat. You won't eat.)	Will you eat?
He/She/It will eat. (He'll/She'll/It'll eat.)	He/She/It will not eat. (He'll/She'll/It'll not eat. He/She/It won't eat.)	Has he/she/it eaten?
We will eat. (We'll eat.)	We will not eat. (We'll not eat. We won't eat.)	Will we eat?
They will eat. (They'll eat.)	They will not eat. (They'll not eat. They won't eat.)	Will they eat?

Note: • The auxiliary *will* is used for all persons.
- In the negative form, contractions can be formed in two different ways.
- In the interrogative form, the auxiliary precedes the subject.
- In the first person singular and plural, *shall* is sometimes used instead of *will* in the interrogative form:
  Shall I eat? Shall we eat?

To transform a yes/no question into an information question, place the question word before the auxiliary:

Will you eat? ➡ ***What** will you eat?*

GRAMMAR TIP
- We use the contracted form of *will* with nouns and interrogative pronouns in spoken English:
  Bob'll be on time. What'll he do?
  Do not use this form in written English.

The *Be Going to* Form
In addition to expressing opinions about the future and making predictions, *be going to* is used to express:

- Prior Plans
  (food, pots and pans are on the kitchen counter)
  *He is going to make supper **in a minute**.*
  (plane tickets have been purchased and hotel reservations made)
  ***Next week**, they are going to fly to Florida for a week's vacation.*

- Imminent Actions
  Slow down! You are going to get a ticket! Didn't you see the police car?

Key Terms

in a minute, next week, next month, next weekend, next year, soon, tonight, etc.

The *be going to* form consists of the present continuous tense of the verb *go* + the full infinitive.

She is going to eat.

Examine *be going to* conjugations in the chart below.

Affirmative	Negative	Interrogative
I am going to eat. (I'm going to eat.)	I am not going to eat. (I'm not going to eat.)	Am I going to eat?
You are going to eat. (You're going to eat.)	You are not going to eat. (You're not going to eat. You aren't going to eat.)	Are you going to eat?
He/She/It is going to eat. (He's/She's/It's going to eat.)	He/She/It is not going to eat. (He's/She's/It's not going to eat. He/She/It isn't going to eat.)	Is he/she/it going to eat?
We are going to eat. (We're going to eat.)	We are not going to eat. (We're not going to eat. We aren't going to eat.)	Are we going to eat?
They are going to eat. (They're going to eat.)	They are not going to eat. (They're not going to eat. They aren't going to eat.)	Are they going to eat?

GRAMMAR TIP
In very informal spoken English, *going to* is pronounced /gonna/. Never use *gonna* in written English.

To transform a yes/no question into an information question, place the question word before the auxiliary:

Is he going to eat? ➡ *Where is he going to eat?*

Would You Like to Practise?

Exercise 1

▬ **Fill in the blanks in the conversation below using either *will* or *be going to*. Do not use contractions. In many instances, either form is possible.**

1. Jason: Do you think that Brian and Susan (start) <u>*will start / are going to start*</u> their family soon?

2. Carl: Yes, they have already told me about their plans: they (have) _____ at least two children.

3. Jason: I predict that he (be) _____ a great father.

4. Jason: I imagine that she (make) _____ a great mother.

5. Carl: Susan told me that she is not able to bear her own children, but this (not stop) _____ them from starting a family.

6. Jason: What (do) _____ they _____?

7. Jason: They (not adopt) _____; that's for sure. Susan has already mentioned that she wants her own biological children.

8. Carl: In that case, they (need) _____ to hire a surrogate mother.

9. Carl: Oh, there's no need to hire anyone. Susan (ask) _____ her twin sister Kate to act as a surrogate.

10. Jason: Do you think Kate (agree) _____?

GRAMMAR TIP
Contractions with question words may be used in spoken English.

Exercise 2

▬ **Fill in the blanks in the conversation below using the contracted form(s) of the words in parentheses.**

1. Susan: Okay, it's all set. (We are) _____*we're*_____ going to have a baby! Kate has agreed to be the surrogate.

2. Susan: She took Dr. O'Malley's number, and (she is) _____ going to call him this afternoon.

3. Brian: You mean (we will not) _____ have to wait any longer?

4. Susan: No! When I told her how much we wanted children, she agreed at once. I hope (we will) _____ soon have a child in the house!

5. Brian: Pass me the phone. (I am going) _____ to call my parents at once.

6. Susan: Well, (I am not going) _____ to call mine.

7. Susan: I have already talked to them about surrogacy, and they don't approve. You do what you want, but (my sister and I are not going) _____ to say a word.

8. Brian: That's crazy! (How will) _____ you explain the pregnancy?

9. Brian: Don't you think (they will) _____ notice?

10. Susan: Okay, you're right. Give me the phone back. (I am) _____ going to call them right now before I lose my nerve!

Exercise 3

■ **Fill in the blanks using either *will* or *be going to*. Do not use contractions. Underline any key words. In many instances, either form is possible.**

1. I (study) ___*am going to study*___ English grammar <u>this afternoon</u>: I've got my books out and all my notes are in order.

2. My friend Julie has agreed to drop by at 3 o'clock: she (help) _____ me study.

3. I imagine she (not arrive) _____ on time. She's always late.

4. She told me she (walk) _____ over to my house.

5. I hope she (not be) _____ too late.

6. Mr. Roberts (give) _____ us a test on Monday. He announced the test last class and told us what to study.

7. I predict the test (be) _____ difficult. His tests always are.

8. My friends David and Mary (fail) _____ probably _____ . They never study.

9. I'm determined to get a great mark. I (study) _____ all afternoon!

10. (Answer) _____ someone _____ the phone? If it's Julie, ask her to bring an English dictionary.

Exercise 4

■ **For each of the statements below, indicate whether an opinion, a prediction, willingness, a promise, a prior plan or an imminent action is being expressed.**

1. I *am going to take* a vacation: I've got my passport, $10,000 and a month off work. _____*prior plan*_____

2. Look out! You *are going to hit* the car in front of us. _____

3. She *is going to go* shopping this afternoon: she's agreed to meet her best friend at the mall at 1 o'clock. _____

4. The phone is ringing. *Will* you *get* it? Sure I *will*. _____

5. The weatherperson predicts it *will rain* all day tomorrow. _____

6. Watch out! You *are going to drive* us off the road. _____

7. They promise they *will be* here on time. _____

8. We *are going to watch* my new DVD tonight: I've called a few friends and they are on their way. _____

9. The palm reader told me, "You *will have* a long and happy life." I hope she's right! _____

10. *Will* you *bring* me a cup of coffee? _____

Exercise 5

■ Transform each of the following affirmative statements into a yes/no question and then into a logical information question with an appropriate answer. (See Appendix A: Common Information Question Words.)

1. It will snow tomorrow.

Yes/No Question	*Will it snow tomorrow?*
Information Question	*When will it snow?*
Answer	*Tomorrow.*

2. The children will behave themselves because they want Santa to leave them lots of presents.

Yes/No Question	
Information Question	
Answer	

3. Their parents will spend thousands of dollars on Christmas gifts.

Yes/No Question	
Information Question	
Answer	

4. They will open all their presents on Christmas Eve.

Yes/No Question	
Information Question	
Answer	

5. They will eat turkey with cranberry sauce.

Yes/No Question	
Information Question	
Answer	

6. The whole family will take a walk on Christmas Day.

Yes/No Question	
Information Question	
Answer	

7. Relatives will call to wish the family a Merry Christmas.

Yes/No Question	
Information Question	
Answer	

8. The family dog will be given a special treat.

Yes/No Question	
Information Question	
Answer	

9. The neighbours will sing Christmas carols.

Yes/No Question	
Information Question	
Answer	

10. They will go to church after supper.

Yes/No Question	
Information Question	
Answer	

Exercise 6

■ Transform each of the following affirmative statements into a yes/no question and then into a logical information question with an appropriate answer. (See Appendix A: Common Information Question Words.)

1. They are going to have another baby in the summer.

Yes/No Question	*Are they going to have another baby?*
Information Question	*When are they going to have another baby?*
Answer	*In the summer.*

2. She is going to give birth at the hospital.

Yes/No Question	
Information Question	
Answer	

3. Her husband is going to be with her in the delivery room.

Yes/No Question	
Information Question	
Answer	

4. Her mother is going to baby-sit her two children.

Yes/No Question	
Information Question	
Answer	

5. They are going to call the baby Samantha.

Yes/No Question	
Information Question	
Answer	

6. Samantha is going to be the couple's first daughter.

Yes/No Question	
Information Question	
Answer	

7. The couple's two sons are going to be very excited when they see Samantha.

Yes/No Question	
Information Question	
Answer	

8. The boys are going to share a bedroom because the new baby needs her own room.

Yes/No Question	
Information Question	
Answer	

9. Friends and family members are going to send gifts for the baby.

Yes/No Question	
Information Question	
Answer	

10. Everyone is going to celebrate the baby's safe arrival.

Yes/No Question	
Information Question	
Answer	

Exercise 7

■ **Fill in the blanks using either *will* or *be going to*. Do not use contractions. In many instances, either form is possible.**

What (do) <u> am </u> I <u> going to do </u> after graduation? Well, I (travel) _____ in the summer and look for work in the fall. I've bought a plane ticket, and I (fly) _____ to Chicago to meet up with an old friend. We've put a deposit on a motor home, and we (drive) _____ down to California. A few friends have agreed to put us up for a couple of weeks: we (stay) _____ with them for a while. Then, we (head up) _____ to Seattle to spend a weekend at a luxury hotel: I've already booked the room! I don't know much about the city, but I am sure it (be) _____ great. Finally, we (drive back) _____ to Chicago. The motor home has to be returned no later than July 15th. I (stay) _____ likely _____ for a week or so before returning to Canada to look for a job. I bought an open-ended plane ticket, so I can stay in Chicago as long as I like. And you, what (do) ^{12.} _____ you ^{13.} _____ after graduation?

Exercise 8

- Write a 50- to 75-word paragraph in which you predict your future. Will you go to university? Will you get married? Will you have children? Will you be rich?
- Use will to make your predictions.

Exercise 9

- Write a 50- to 75-word paragraph in which you discuss some plans you have made. What are you going to do next summer? What university are you going to attend? Where are you going to travel?
- Use the *be going to* form.

Exercise 10

- Correct each of the sentences below.

1. When will he ~~gets~~ here?

Correction(s): *get* _____

2. They going to be here any minute.

Correction(s): _____

3. When Robert will drop by?

Correction(s): _____

4. We wo'nt know until we try.

Correction(s): _____

5. I predict he going to be late.

Correction(s): _____

6. I'm sure Martin'll and Sandra'll be here soon.

Correction(s): _____

7. I am going work very hard.

Correction(s): _____

8. Your boss is going to show up?

Correction(s): _____

9. Watch out! That tree will fall on your head.

Correction(s): _____

10. Is he gonna be late?

Correction(s): _____

Would You Like to Talk about It?

Activity 1: Sharing Opinions and Making Predictions
This activity is designed to help you practise using *will* and/or *be going to* with a partner.

Required
• Sentence Completions Worksheet (below)

Instructions
1. Read and complete the worksheet with the first thing that pops into you mind. Remember to use *will* or *be going to*.
2. Student A begins, reading the first sentence completion to Student B.
3. Student B asks a question, preferably in the simple future.
   Example: Student A: *I believe that my generation will make a difference!*
   Student B: *How will it make a difference?*
4. Student B continues, reading the first sentence completion to Student A.
5. Student A asks a question, preferably in the simple future.
   Example: Student B: *I hope that world hunger will end.*
   Student A: *How many years will it take?*
6. Repeat steps 2–5 until all the sentence completions have been read, and the questions have been asked and answered.

Suggestion: Exchange sentence completions and repeat the activity.

Sentence Completions Worksheet

Student A
1. I hope that _____

_____

2. I fear that _____

_____

3. I doubt that _____

_____

4. In the next 20 years, I am sure that _____

_____

5. I predict that _____

_____

Student B

1. I expect that _____

_____

2. I believe that _____

_____

3. I assume that _____

_____

4. In the next five years, I am convinced that _____

_____

4. I think that _____

_____

Activity 2: Miming

In this activity, you will use *be going to* for prior plans and imminent actions.
This activity works best in groups of 6–8.

Required
- Imminent Actions List (see below)
- 20 slips of paper
- A hat (or small container)

Instructions
1. As a group, write each of the imminent actions on a separate slip of paper.
2. Put all slips of paper in a hat (or small container).
3. Form two teams, approximately equal in number.
4. One member from Team 1 selects a slip of paper and proceeds to mime the activities leading up to the imminent action **but not the action itself**. Example: A member miming the actions leading up to "you are going to ride a bike" would mime unlocking the bike, putting on a helmet, adjusting the seat, etc., but would not mime riding a bike.
5. The other members of Team 1 have one minute to guess the imminent action. If they correctly guess what their teammate "is going to do," the team gets a point. If not, no point is awarded.
6. One member from Team 2 selects a slip of paper and proceeds to mime the activities leading up to the imminent action described.

7. The other members of Team 2 have one minute to guess the imminent action. If they correctly guess what their teammate "is going to do," the team gets a point. If not, no point is awarded.

8. Repeat steps 4–7 until all the slips of paper have been used.

Suggestion: Repeat the activity using your own list of imminent actions. To make the activity more challenging, Team 1 creates a list of imminent actions for Team 2 and vice versa.

Imminent Actions List	
1. You are going to shave.	11. You are going to parachute from a plane.
2. You are going to open a bottle of wine.	12. You are going to paint your bedroom.
3. You are going to walk the dog.	13. You are going to cook an omelette.
4. You are going to feed the baby his/her bottle.	14. You are going to play hockey.
5. You are going to iron your clothes.	15. You are going to change the baby's diaper.
6. You are going to mow the lawn.	16. You are going to do the laundry.
7. You are going to do your homework.	17. You are going to wash the floor.
8. You are going to go jogging.	18. You are going to order lunch.
9. You are going to heat up some soup.	19. You are going to take a shower.
10. You are going to change a flat tire.	20. You are going to watch a DVD.

What Is Your Mood?

Modal auxiliaries, also known as modals, are special verbs used along with other verbs to express a particular *mood*.

> *Alexandre Despatie* **can** *dive superbly.* (ability)
> *The government* **should** *negotiate with its workers.* (advisability)

In this unit, we will examine some of the more common modals.

If *you're* in the mood, let's get started!

Did You Know?

Modals can be used to express:

- Ability
  She **can** *cook well.*
  He **could** *jog for miles when he was a teenager.* (Past)

- Advisability
  He **should** *apologize to her today.*

- Obligation
  You **must** *be on time.*
  You **have** *to be on time.* (Informal)
  You **had** *to be on time.* (Past)

- Possibility
  They **may** *study tonight.*
  He **might** *do his homework.*
  John **could** *call tomorrow morning.*

- Logical conclusion
  Someone is at the door. Oh, that **must** *be Harold.*

- Preference
  I **would rather** *have steak than chicken.*

The simple form of the verb directly follows most modal auxiliaries. In such a case, the modal auxiliary is the same for all persons.

I can sing.
You can sing.
He/She/It can sing.
We can sing.
They can sing.

> **GRAMMAR TIP**
> Modals have no particular time sense. *Could* may be used to express the present, and it may be used to express the past.
> *I* **could** *study tonight.*
> *I* **could** *study for hours when I was a student.*

Examine the chart below.

Function	Affirmative	Negative	Interrogative
Ability can could (past)	He can skate. He could skate.	He cannot (can't) skate. He could not (couldn't) skate.	Can he skate? Could he skate?
Advisability should	She should pay.	She should not (shouldn't) pay.	Should she pay?
Obligation must have to (informal)	I must pay my bills.	I do not (don't) have to pay my bills. He does not (doesn't) have to pay his bills.	Must I pay my bills? Do I have to pay my bills? Does he have to pay his bills?
had to (past)	I had to pay the fine.	I did not (didn't) have to pay the fine.	Did I have to pay the fine?
Possibility may might could	It may be sunny. It might rain. It could snow.	It may not be sunny. It might not rain.	Might it rain? Could it snow?
Logical Conclusion must	That must be Carole at the door.	That must not (mustn't) be Carole at the door.	Must that be Carole at the door?
Preference would rather	They would rather eat pizza.	They would rather not eat pizza.	Would they rather eat pizza?

Note:
• To express ability in the past, use *could*.
• To express a lack of obligation in the present, use *do/does not have to*.
• To express obligation in the past, use *had to*.
• To express a negative possibility, only use *may not* or *might not*. To ask about possibility, only use *might* or *could*.
• The contractions *mayn't* and *mightn't* are rarely used.

To transform a yes/no question into an information question, place the question word before the auxiliary:

Should he apologize? ➡ **Why** *should he apologize?*

Modals may also be used to make and respond to polite requests.

Requests with *I* or *we* as the subject	Requests with *you* as the subject
May I (or we) leave? Yes, you may. No, you may not.	*Would* you explain this to me? Yes, I ~~would~~ will. No, I ~~would~~ will not.
Might I (or we) be excused? Yes, you ~~might~~ may. No, you ~~might~~ may not.	*Will* you show me how to do this? Yes, I will. No, I will not.
Could I (or we) go? Yes, you ~~could~~ may. No, you ~~could~~ may not.	*Could* you repeat that, please? Yes, I ~~could~~ will. No, I ~~could~~ will not

Exercise 1

▬ Write about activities you could do in the past but cannot do now.

1. *When I was a young child, I could do a cartwheel. I cannot (can't) do that now.* _____

2. _____
   _____

3. _____
   _____

4. _____
   _____

5. _____
   _____

Exercise 2

▬ Give advice for each of the problems below.

1. Brian is not feeling well.
   Advice: *Brian should go see a doctor.* _____

2. Mihran is failing his math course.
   Advice: _____

3. Mien Chien has insomnia.
   Advice: _____

4. Carl is afraid to ask Melinda out on a date.
   Advice: _____

5. Carlos doesn't speak English very well.

Advice: _____

6. Valerie doesn't have a summer job.

Advice: _____

7. Annabelle is afraid to give a presentation in English.

Advice: _____

8. Justin doesn't know what he wants to do in life.

Advice: _____

9. Michael is unhappy living with his parents.

Advice: _____

10. Anthony is feeling tired and he has no energy.

Advice: _____

Exercise 3

■ **Write about obligations you have today and obligations you don't have today. Then, write about obligations you had last week and obligations you didn't have last week.**

Obligation

  1. Today, *I must do my grammar exercises.* _____

  2. Today, _____

  3. Today, _____

Lack of obligation

  4. Today, _____

  5. Today, _____

Obligation

  6. Last week, _____

  7. Last week, _____

  8. Last week, _____

Lack of obligation

  9. Last week, _____

  10. Last week, _____

Exercise 4

■ Write about possibilities for next week, next month, next year, and five years from now. Then, negate each of the sentences you have written.

1. Tomorrow, *I might have friends over for supper.*
   Negation: *I might not have friends over for supper.*

2. Next week, _____
   Negation: _____

3. Next month, _____
   Negation: _____

4. Next year, _____
   Negation: _____

5. Five years from now, _____
   Negation: _____

Exercise 5

■ Write one affirmative logical conclusion and one negative logical conclusion on the present for each of the scenarios below.

1. Steve didn't eat anything on his plate.
   Affirmative logical conclusion: *He must be on a diet.*
   Negative logical conclusion: *He must not be hungry.*

2. Marguerite works out at the gym five times a week.
   Affirmative logical conclusion: _____
   Negative logical conclusion: _____

3. Greg is smiling.
   Affirmative logical conclusion: _____
   Negative logical conclusion: _____

4. Keith ate three bags of potato chips.
   Affirmative logical conclusion: _____
   Negative logical conclusion: _____

5. Sylvia hasn't mowed her lawn in a month.
   Affirmative logical conclusion: _____
   Negative logical conclusion: _____

Exercise 6

■ **State your preference. Choose from each of the following options.**

1. Be unhealthy and rich. Be healthy and poor.
   I would rather be healthy and poor than unhealthy and rich!

2. Be extremely attractive. Be extremely intelligent.
   _____

3. Watch TV. Play on the computer.
   _____

4. Go to the beach. Hike in the mountains.
   _____

5. Take someone out for an expensive meal. Be taken out for an expensive meal.
   _____

6. Be popular. Be respected.
   _____

7. Have 12 children. Have no children.
   _____

8. Win $1,000 a week for life. Win $20,000,000.
   _____

9. Be a cat. Be a dog.
   _____

10. Live in the country. Live in the city.
    _____

Exercise 7

■ **Transform each of the following into polite requests.**

1. Get me a cup of coffee. ➡ *Could you get me a cup of coffee?*

2. I'm getting something to eat. ➡ *May I get something to eat?*

3. Leave the classroom! ➡ _____

4. Spell that for me. ➡ _____

5. We are going home early. ➡ _____

6. Shut the window. ➡ _____

7. Lend me some money. ➡ _____

8. Stop interrupting. ➡ _____

9. I'm taking twenty dollars out of your purse. ➡ _____

_____

10. Be quiet. ➡ _____

Exercise 8

▬ **Underline the correct modal in parentheses.**

Every day, Canadians are dying because they (<u>cannot</u>, must not, should not) get a kidney transplant. There are too many patients and not enough organs. People really (may, should, might) sign their organ donation cards. With many patients dying on waiting lists, Canadians (had to, would rather, must) realize how important organ donation is by now!

There are many possibilities as to why people don't donate. They (should, had to, could) be afraid to face their own mortality. They (must not, might not, should not) like to think about a surgeon removing vital organs. They (should, have to, may even) just be selfish! Who knows?

The government absolutely (must, should, had to) impress upon the population the importance of donating. People (should, can, must) make a difference—if they want to!

Personally, I (would, would rather, could rather) die knowing I'd helped someone than knowing I could have helped but didn't.

Exercise 9

▬ **Write a 50- to 75-word paragraph on any topic you wish in which you will use at least three of the following modals: can, should, must, may, might, could, must, or would rather.**

Exercise 10

▬ **Correct each of the sentences below.**

1. ~~He should~~ tell her the truth?

Correction(s): *Should he* _____

2. He cann't be there on time.

Correction(s): _____

3. People must to sign their organ donation cards.

   Correction(s): _____

4. She would donate a kidney to her cousin than let him continue with dialysis.

   Correction(s): _____

5. I mustn't have to pay my taxes.

   Correction(s): _____

6. He can to have a cup of coffee?

   Correction(s): _____

7. May you answer my question?

   Correction(s): _____

8. Why he should apologize?

   Correction(s): _____

9. They had pay their bills yesterday.

   Correction(s): _____

10. Perhaps it could not snow tomorrow.

    Correction(s): _____

Would You Like to Talk about It?

Activity 1: Preferences

This activity is designed to help you practise the modal structure *would rather* to discuss preferences. Work in pairs.

Required
• This textbook

Instructions
1. Go back to Exercise 6 in this unit.
2. Student A questions Student B about Student B's odd-numbered answers (1, 3, 5, 7 and 9). For example:
   Student A: *Why would you rather be healthy and poor than unhealthy and rich?*
3. Student B explains his/her choice.
4. Student B questions Student A about Student A's even-numbered answers (2, 4, 6, 8 and 10). For example:
   Student B : *Why would you rather be intelligent than attractive?*
5. Student A explains his/her choice.

6. Alternate questions until all ten questions have been asked and the preferences have been explained.

Suggestion: Repeat the activity, exchanging questions. Student A asks the even-numbered questions and Student B asks the odd-numbered questions.

Activity 2: What Should I Do?

This activity is designed to help you practise using *should* for advisability. This activity works best with teams of four to six members.

Required
- 3 slips of paper for each member of the group
- A hat (or small container)

Instructions
1. Each member writes down three problems, one on each slip of paper. For example, "I am out of shape."
2. All the members put their slips of paper (their problems) in a hat (or small container).
3. The member whose first name is closest to the letter A begins. He/she draws a slip of paper and reads the problem aloud. After reading the problem, he/she asks the group, "What should I do?"
4. Team members give Player 1 some advice.
5. Player 1 awards the paper to the person who (in Player 1's opinion) has offered the most creative piece of advice.
6. This player in turn takes a slip of paper from the hat (or small container). He/she asks the other players for advice and awards the slip of paper to the person who has offered the most creative piece of advice.
7. The game continues in this way until all the slips of paper have been selected and awarded to the most creative advice-givers.
8. The player with the most slips of paper at the end of the game is declared the winner.

Suggestion: Use "real" problems if you can. In addition to having fun, you might actually solve some of the group members' problems!

Is It Conditional?

Picture it! You buy a lottery ticket, and the grand prize is 20 million dollars.

- Your ticket numbers? 1, 2, 3, 4, 5 and 6.
- The first number comes up: it is a 1.
- The second number comes up: it is a 2.
- The third number comes up: it is a 3.

By this time, you're excitedly thinking about all the wonderful things you will buy if you win:

> ***If I win, I will buy*** *a big house … a fast car … a trip around the world …*

Of course, the next three numbers are 7, 8 and 9—and now you're thinking:

> ***If I had won, I would have bought*** *a big house … a fast car … a trip around the world …*

Some people never buy lottery tickets, but they still like to dream about what they would buy if they won:

> ***If I won, I would buy*** *a big house … a fast car … a trip around the world …*

In this unit, we are going to examine the three conditionals described above:

1. The present real (*If I win, I will buy…*)
2. The present unreal (*If I won, I would buy…*)
3. The past unreal (*If I had won, I would have bought …*)

If you're ready, we'll begin!

Did You Know?

A conditional has an **if-clause** and a result clause. The most common conditionals can be classified as follows:

1. The Present Real Conditional
If Sonia listens to the teacher, she will get great marks.
(Sonia will probably listen to her teacher, so great marks are to be expected.)

The present real conditional is used to talk about real present/future situations, as the action in the if-clause is quite *probable*.

2. The Present Unreal Conditional

If John listened to the teacher, he would get great marks.
(John will probably not listen to his teacher, so great marks are not to be expected.)

The present unreal conditional is used to talk about unreal present/future situations, as the action in the if-clause is *improbable* or *imaginary*.

3. The Past Unreal Conditional

If Adam and Christine had listened to the teacher, they would have gotten great marks.
(Adam and Christine did not listen to the teacher, so great marks were not obtained.)

The past unreal conditional is used to talk about unreal past situations, as the action in the if-clause did not occur. The situation is purely *hypothetical*.

> **GRAMMAR TIP**
> Use the present real conditional for probable situations.
> Use the present unreal conditional for improbable or imaginary situations.
> Use the past unreal conditional for hypothetical situations.

Examine the chart below.

Conditionals	If-Clauses	Result Clauses
Present Real	If he studies, simple present	he will (he'll) succeed. subject + **will** + simple form of the verb
Present Unreal	If he studied, simple past	he would (he'd) succeed. subject + **would** + simple form of the verb
Past Unreal	If he had (he'd) studied, past perfect	he would (he'd) have succeeded. subject + **would have** + past participle

Note: • Never use the simple future in an if-clause:
If he ~~will study~~ studies, he will succeed.
• Even though the simple past is used in the if-clause of the present unreal conditional, the situation being discussed is in the present/future.
• The past perfect is formed with *had* and the past participle:
He had eaten.
They had driven.
• The negative form may be used in either—or both—clauses:
If he does not study hard, he will not succeed.
If he did not study hard, his father would be upset.
If he had studied hard, his father would not have been disappointed in him.

> **GRAMMAR TIP**
> When conjugating *be* in the if-clause of the present unreal conditional, use *were* for all persons when using formal English:
>
> *If Jane ~~was~~ were here, we could start the party.*
> *Were* is a subjunctive form.

To form interrogative sentences, invert the subject and the auxiliary in the result clause.

1. *If he studies, he will succeed.* ➡ *If he studies, **will he** succeed?*

2. *If he studied, he would succeed.* ➡ *If he studied, **would he** succeed?*

3. *If he had studied, he would have succeeded.* ➡ *If he had studied, **would he** have succeeded?*

> **GRAMMAR TIP**
> If you place the result clause before the if-clause, remove the comma.
> *If he studies, he will succeed.* ➡ *He will succeed if he studies.*

Conditionals with Modals

The result clause of a conditional can contain a modal (see Unit 6). Refer to the chart below for examples.

Conditionals	Examples with Modals
Present Real	• Result clause with *may, can, must* or *should* If she is hungry, she **may** eat my lunch. (permission) If he burns supper, we **can** eat out. (possibility) If his stomach is gurgling, he **must** be hungry. (logical conclusion) If we are served well, we **should** leave a good tip. (advisability)
Present Unreal	• Result clause with *could* or *might* If she knew his name, she **could** call him. (present ability) If she asked him out, he **might** accept. (present possibility)
Past Unreal	Result clause with *could have* or *might have* If she had known his name, she **could have** called him. (past ability) If she had asked him out, he **might have** accepted. (past possibility)

 Would You Like to Practise?

Exercise 1

▬ **Write sentences in the present real conditional using the words in parentheses. Use the words in the order they appear.**

1. (I / exercise / I / lose weight) *If I exercise, I will lose weight.*

2. (Karen and Bob / get a week off / they / go to Mexico) _____

_____

3. (the little boy / do not eat on time / he / cry) _____
_____

4. (he / eat "poutine" every day / he / get fat) _____
_____

5. (the dogs / hear a noise / they / bark) _____
_____

6. (I / want to / I / buy myself something nice) _____
_____

7. (you / be not very good / you / lose your job) _____
_____

8. (he / have enough money / he / take us out for supper) _____
_____

9. (they / sit together / they / laugh throughout the course) _____
_____

10. (she / save enough money / she / take a trip) _____
_____

Exercise 2

■ **Write sentences in the present unreal conditional using the words in parentheses. Use the words in the order they appear.**

1. (she / be nicer / she / have more friends) *If she were nicer, she would* _____
have more friends. _____

2. (she / find a wallet / she / return it) _____
_____

3. (the weather / be warmer / we / go to the beach) _____
_____

4. (Kate and Karen / study harder / they / pass the course) _____
_____

5. (the dog / run away / his owner / be very upset) _____
_____

6. (her son / give her a present on her birthday / she / be very surprised)

_____

7. (Mike and Dan / paint the house all night / they / finish in the morning)

_____

8. (I / have a million dollars / I / quit my job) _____

_____

9. (the government / cut taxes / Canadians / be richer) _____

_____

10. (the Canadian dollar / be stronger / Canadians / travel more) _____

_____

Exercise 3

➡ **Write sentences in the past unreal conditional using the words in parentheses. Use the words in the order they appear.**

1. (I / work harder / I / got a better job) _If I had worked harder, I would_ _____ _have gotten a better job._ _____

2. (the fire / not destroy her home / she / not apply for welfare) _____

_____

3. (Steve / not fail all his courses / he / attend university) _____

_____

4. (her boyfriend / not cheat on her / she / not break up with him) _____

_____

5. (Cindy / not tell her parents the truth / she / feel guilty) _____

_____

6. (I / tell her the truth / she / forgive me) _____

_____

7. (Philippe and Christine / talk more / they / not break up) _____

_____

8. (Harold / have a car accident / he / tell his wife) _____

_____

9. (the police officer / not give me a ticket / I / be in a better mood) _____

_____

10. (the class / not do well on the test / the teacher / give a make-up test) ___

_____

Exercise 4

■ **Match each of the following if-clauses with an appropriate result clause. The first one has been done for you.**

If-Clauses		Result Clauses
1. If it rains,	g	a. the picnic would be cancelled.
2. If it rained,		b. their children will be upset.
3. If it had rained,		c. the researchers would not have lost their jobs.
4. If Ken and Martha get a divorce,		d. you will have to make it up in summer school.
5. If John quit his job,		e. his girlfriend would not have left him.
6. If you don't pass the course,		f. the researchers would not lose their jobs.
7. If Kevin had apologized,		g. the picnic will be cancelled.
8. If the experiment had worked,		h. the researchers will not lose their jobs.
9. If the experiment worked,		i. the company would be losing a good employee.
10. If the experiment works,		j. the picnic would have been cancelled.

Exercise 5

■ **Fill in the blanks using the correct form of the verb in parentheses.**

1. If people truly (care) _____*cared*_____ about animals, they would stop all animal experimentation.

2. If scientists (experiment) _____ on animals first, the findings can be used to save human lives.

3. Scientists (notify) _____ the public immediately if the virus had spread to other patients.

4. If no human organs (be) _____ available, would you allow doctors to transplant an animal organ into your body?

5. If the government (permit) _____ xenotransplantations, animal-to-human transplants must be safe.

6. If researchers find a solution, (give) _____ they _____ it away for free?

7. If one species (become) _____ extinct, will other species follow?

8. I (have) _____ a xenotransplantation if no human organs were available.

9. She would have donated money for research if you (ask) _____ her.

10. If an alternate solution (exist) _____, should we continue sacrificing animals to save human lives?

Exercise 6

■ **Complete each of the conditionals below by adding an appropriate result clause.**

1. If xenotransplantation techniques are improved, *more lives will be saved.*

_____

2. If I had diabetes, _____

_____

3. If I needed an animal organ to save my life, _____

_____

4. If the operation is too dangerous, _____

_____

5. If either of my parents needed an organ donation, _____

_____

6. If researchers are successful, _____

_____

7. If the scientist had known about the risk, _____

_____

8. If animal experimentation is banned, _____

_____

9. If animal experimentation were banned, _____

_____

10. If animal experimentation had been banned, _____

_____

Exercise 7

■ **Create an if-clause for each of the following result clauses.**

1. Lives could be saved *if people wore their seat belts.* _____

   _____

2. I could buy anything I wanted _____

   _____

3. She will get into Harvard _____

   _____

4. I could have gotten a better grade _____

   _____

5. They would have gotten married _____

6. Kate will tell Kevin the truth _____

   _____

7. My school would be a better place _____

   _____

8. He should review his grammar notes _____

   _____

9. War would end _____

   _____

10. Last year would have been better _____

    _____

Exercise 8

■ **Fill in the blanks using the correct form of the verb in parentheses. Do not use contractions.**

Some people spend all of their lives "regretting." Have you ever met such people? They'll say things like, "If I (work) ^{1.}_____ harder in school, I would have gotten a better job." "If I hadn't been so hard to live with, she (not leave) ^{2.}_____ me." "If my parents (be) ^{3.}_____ more loving, I would have been more successful."

I understand that it's tempting to dwell on the past, but this doesn't do anybody any good.

People need to focus on solutions, not problems.

Instead of complaining about being overweight, people should simply focus on how to lose the excess weight. If they (want) <u>   ^{4.}   </u> to lose weight, they can join a gym, they can go on a diet or they can walk a mile every day. There are many possibilities.

If I (be) <u>   ^{5.}   </u> a "regretter," I would stop looking back and start looking forward.

Exercise 9

■ Write a 50- to 75-word paragraph in which you describe what you would do if you won 20 million dollars.

Exercise 10

■ Correct each of the sentences below.

1. If I ~~win~~ the lottery, I would buy a new house.
   Correction(s): <u>*won*   </u>

2. If my parents won the lottery, they would have given me some money.
   Correction(s): _____

3. If they had work harder, they would have done better.
   Correction(s): _____

4. If her boss would give her a promotion, she would have more money.
   Correction(s): _____

5. If people are kinder, the world would be a better place.
   Correction(s): _____

6. If she knew, she would have told me.
   Correction(s): _____

7. They will come to the party if you invited them.
   Correction(s): _____

8. They will go to Mexico at Christmas if their boss will give them a bonus this year.
   Correction(s): _____

9. If she will study, she will do well in the course.

Correction(s): _____

10. Carla and Carole would come to the picnic if you invite them.

Correction(s): _____

Would You Like to Talk about It?

Activity 1: Giving Advice

Work with a partner to practise giving advice, using the present real and unreal conditionals.

Required
• A couple of sheets of lined paper, a pen or a pencil

Instructions
1. On a sheet of lined paper, both partners write down five realistic objectives they want to accomplish in the future. Examples:

I want to get more than 90 percent on my next math test.
I want to become a doctor.
I want to get a part-time job.
I want to travel across Europe.
I want to complete the Montreal marathon.

2. On the same sheet of paper, both partners write down five problems they have right now. Examples:

I don't understand my math homework.
I don't have a boyfriend/girlfriend.
I don't have money to pay my bills.
I have insomnia.
I am always late for class.

3. Student A reads one of his/her objectives to Student B. Student B gives some advice on how to attain the objective, beginning with "If you want to _____, you should _____."

4. Student A continues, reading one of his/her problems to Student B. Student B gives some advice on how to solve the problem, beginning with "If I were you, I would _____."

5. Student B reads one of his/her objectives to Student A. Student A gives some advice on how to attain the objective, beginning with "If you want to _____, you should _____."

6. Student B continues, reading one of his/her problems to Student A. Student A gives some advice on how to solve the problem, beginning with "If I were you, I would _____."

7. Repeat steps three to six until all the objectives and problems have been read and responded to with advice.

Suggestion: Don't be afraid to "reject" the advice you hear, encouraging your partner to come up with alternative solutions. In this way, you will get more practice using the present real and unreal conditionals.

Activity 2: Conditional Clauses

This activity is designed to help you practise all three conditionals: the present real and unreal and the past unreal. You will need two teams of two or three players for this activity.

Required
- 30 slips of paper, 15 for each team
- A pair of scissors
- 2 hats or small containers
- A timer

Instructions
1. Each team writes down 15 sentences, 5 in the present real, 5 in the present unreal and 5 in the past unreal. Examples:

   If Jane eats a big breakfast, she won't be hungry by mid-morning.
   If I won a lot of money, I would give some of it to my brother.
   If it had snowed, I would have gone skiing.

   Each of the 15 sentences must be written on a separate sheet of paper.

2. Each team cuts its 15 conditional sentences in two, separating the if-clauses from the result clauses.
3. Each team places all 30 clauses in a hat (or small container), mixes them up and exchanges hats (or small containers) with the opposing team.
4. The first team to reconstruct correctly all 15 conditional sentences is declared the winner.

Suggestion: Any conditional sentence that is grammatically correct (the tenses are paired correctly) and "makes sense" (even if the reconstructed sentence is not the original sentence) should be accepted. If necessary, ask your teacher to act as the referee.

Which Voice Do You Want to Use?

Verbs can be expressed in either the passive or the active voice.

Active	Passive
Lisa Fitterman *wrote* the article.	The article *was written* by Lisa Fitterman.
You *must submit* the assignment on time.	The assignment *must be submitted* on time.

In the active voice, the subject (Lisa Fitterman/you) "acts": the subject is active.

In the passive voice, the subject (article/assignment) "is acted upon": the subject is passive.

In this unit, our attention will be focused on the verb tenses and forms studied in units two to six of this textbook. (Did you notice that the last sentence was written in the passive voice?) Verbs can be expressed in either the passive or the active voice.

 Did You **Know?**

In general, the passive voice is used when the performer of the action is:

• Unimportant
The lawn was mowed.

• Unknown
The necklace has been stolen.

To make an active sentence passive:
1. Identify the verb tense of the active verb.
2. Conjugate *be* in the same tense as the active verb.
3. Add the past participle of the active verb.

*Andrew **is making** the dinner.* (Active)
➡ *The dinner **is being made** by Andrew.* (Passive)

Note:
• The active verb is in the present continuous tense.
• *Be* in the present continuous tense = *is being*.
• The past participle of *make* = *made*.

The object of the active sentence (the dinner) becomes the subject in the passive sentence.

> **GRAMMAR TIP**
> For modals in the passive voice, use the base form *be* followed by the past participle:
> *They **must** do their work.* ➡ *Their work **must be done**.*

Look at the chart below for examples of the active and passive voices in different verb tenses and modal forms. Each example has the affirmative, negative and interrogative forms.

Verb Tenses/Forms	Active Voice	Passive Voice
Simple present	She *sends* a cheque every month.	A cheque *is sent* every month.
	He *does not (doesn't) send* a reply.	A reply *is not (isn't) sent.*
	Do they *discuss* the problem?	*Is* the problem *discussed?*
Present continuous	The thief *is hiding* the cash.	The cash *is being hidden.*
	The police *are not (aren't) arresting* the thief.	The thief *is not (isn't) being arrested.*
	Are the police *handcuffing* the thief?	*Is* the thief *being handcuffed?*
Simple past	We *took* the dog for a walk.	The dog *was taken* for a walk.
	We *did not (didn't) leash* the dog.	The dog *was not (wasn't) leashed.*
	Did they *feed* the dog?	*Was* the dog *fed?*
Past continuous	He *was doing* the homework.	The homework *was being done.*
	He *was not (wasn't) writing* a report.	A report *was not (wasn't) being written.*
	Was he *revising* the essay?	*Was* the essay *being revised?*
Present perfect	Steven *has paid* the bill.	The bill *has been paid.*
	The chef *has not (hasn't) made* lunch.	Lunch *has not (hasn't) been made.*
	Has someone *washed* the dishes?	*Have* the dishes *been washed?*
Future • With *will* • The *be going to* form	They *will sell* the house. They *are going to sell* the house.	The house *will be sold.* The house *is going to be sold.*
	We *will not (won't) rent* the condo. We *are not (aren't) going to rent* the condo.	The condo *will not (won't) be rented.* The condo *is not (isn't) going to be rented.*
	Will he *give away* the money? *Is* he *going to give away* the money?	*Will* the money *be given away?* *Is* the money *going to be given away?*
Modals	He *might donate* some money.	Some money *might be donated.*
	She *could offer* some help.	Some help *could be offered.*
	Must they *raise* a lot of money?	*Must* a lot of money *be raised?*

Note: • Form the passive with *be* and the past participle of the verb.
(If you are unsure of the past participle of an irregular verb, refer to the verb chart in Appendix B.)
• In the passive interrogative form, the auxiliary precedes the subject.

GRAMMAR TIP
Only verbs that take direct objects can be used in the passive because the direct object becomes the subject of the passive sentence:

Sylvester walked to the store. ➡ ~~*The store was walked to by Sylvester.*~~

GRAMMAR TIP
The passive voice may
be used with *by* to *stress*
the importance of the
performer of the action.
For example:

*The report was completed
by Jason—not Andrew!*

To transform a yes/no question into an information question, place the question word before the auxiliary:

Was the dog fed? ➡ **When** *was the dog fed?*

Would You Like to Practise?

Exercise 1

■ **For each of the active sentences below, indicate which of the following tenses is being used: simple present; present continuous; simple past; past continuous; present perfect; or future (*will* or the *be going to* form). If a modal is used, simply write "modal form."**

1. Parliament *might legalize* euthanasia in the near future.	*modal form*
2. Canadians *have* strong opinions on the issue.	
3. Sue Rodriguez *fought* for the legalization of assisted suicide.	
4. Many people with terminal diseases *are fighting* against the legalization of assisted suicide.	
5. *Will* euthanasia ever be legalized?	
6. Who *is going to protect* patients from potential abuse?	
7. While the Supreme Court of Canada *was hearing* arguments for and against assisted suicide, demonstrators *were protesting* throughout the nation.	
8. Many Canadians *have written* living wills.	
9. *Should* doctors *have* the right to assist a patient's suicide?	
10. Where *do* you *stand* on the issue?	

Exercise 2

■ **Indicate whether each of the verbs in italics is in the active or the passive voice. The first one has been done for you.**

1. The term "euthanasia" *is derived* from the Greek words "eu" and "thanatos."   Active ☐ Passive ☑

2. Euthanasia *can be divided* into two categories: voluntary and nonvoluntary.   Active ☐ Passive ☐

3. In Canada, the distinction between passive and active euthanasia *is* important.   Active ☐ Passive ☐

4. We *will focus* our attention on voluntary active euthanasia.   Active ☐ Passive ☐

5. You *will be asked* to consider both sides of the active euthanasia debate.   Active ☐ Passive ☐

6. Who *owns* your life?   Active ☐ Passive ☐

7. *Is* life a gift?   Active ☐ Passive ☐

8. What *has* he *been told* about his illness?   Active ☐ Passive ☐

9. Euthanasia *has been debated* for decades.   Active ☐ Passive ☐

10. How long *should* society *debate* the question before finally making a decision?   Active ☐ Passive ☐

Exercise 3

■ **If possible, rewrite the simple present and present continuous sentences below in the passive voice.**

Reminder: To make an active sentence passive, the verb must take a direct object. Not all of the sentences can be rewritten.

1. Ken and Louise are building a house.
    Passive: *A house is being built (by Ken and Louise).*

2. Louise is hooking up the electricity.
    Passive: _____

3. Ken is painting the kitchen.
    Passive: _____

4. Louise decides to take a break.
    Passive: _____

5. Ken doesn't want to stop.
    Passive: _____

6. Ken paints the ceiling.
    Passive: _____

7. Louise makes some coffee.

Passive: _____

8. Ken and Louise are building a very expensive house.

Passive: _____

9. Ken and Louise are using only the best materials.

Passive: _____

10. Ken and Louise are working very hard.

Passive: _____

Exercise 4

■ Correct each of the statements below. Write your corrections in the passive voice. Use *by* followed by the name of the person (in parentheses) who actually made the achievement.

1. Frank Lloyd Wright designed the Eiffel Tower. (Gustave Eiffel)

Correction(s): *The Eiffel Tower was designed by Gustave Eiffel.* _____

2. Antoine Dessane composed the music for the anthem "O Canada." (Calixa Lavallée)

Correction(s): _____

3. Dr. Wilder Penfield discovered insulin. (Frederick Banting and Charles Best)

Correction(s): _____

4. Le Corbusier drew up the plans for the World Trade Center. (Minoru Yamasaki)

Correction(s): _____

5. Margaret Atwood wrote the novel *Kamouraska*. (Anne Hébert)

Correction(s): _____

6. Marie Currie was developing the law of the photoelectric effect in 1905. (Albert Einstein)

Correction(s): *In 1905,* _____

7. Rembrandt painted the Mona Lisa. (Leonardo da Vinci)

Correction(s): _____

8. Rick Hanson was raising money for cancer research in 1980. (Terry Fox)

Correction(s): _In 1980,_ _____

9. In 1992, Sarah McLachlan won the Grammy for the song "Constant Craving". (k.d. lang)

Correction(s): _In 1992,_ _____

10. The Detroit Red Wings won the Stanley Cup in 2003. (the New Jersey Devils)

Correction(s): _In 2003,_ _____

Exercise 5

- Transform each of the following passive statements in the present perfect into a yes/no question.
- Write an information question that corresponds to the words in italics, and then answer the question.

1. The patient has been given _a painkiller_.

Yes/No Question	_Has the patient been given a painkiller?_
Information Question	_What has the patient been given?_
Answer	_A painkiller._

2. HIV has been _successfully_ treated.

Yes/No Question	
Information Question	
Answer	

3. Her grandmother has been diagnosed with _Alzheimer's Disease_.

Yes/No Question	
Information Question	
Answer	

4. She has been hospitalized _because she cannot care for herself_.

Yes/No Question	
Information Question	
Answer	

5. Robert Latimer has been condemmed *for killing his daughter Tracy*.

Yes/No Question	
Information Question	
Answer	

6. *Robert Latimer's conviction* has been appealed.

Yes/No Question	
Information Question	
Answer	

7. Doctor-assisted suicide has been legalized *in Holland*.

Yes/No Question	
Information Question	
Answer	

8. *Elderly Dutch* patients have been pressured to end their lives.

Yes/No Question	
Information Question	
Answer	

9. She has been kept *artificially* alive.

Yes/No Question	
Information Question	
Answer	

10. Euthanasia has been debated in Canada *for many years*.

Yes/No Question	
Information Question	
Answer	

Exercise 6

■ **Rewrite the sentences with *will* and *be going to* in the passive voice.**

Reminder: To make an active sentence passive, the verb must take a direct object. Not all of the sentences can be rewritten.

1. Canada will legalize euthanasia one day.

Passive: *Euthanasia will be legalized in Canada one day.*

2. Canadians will demand change.

   Passive: _____

3. Many people are going to debate the issue.

   Passive: _____

4. The debate will be heated.

   Passive: _____

5. Some doctors will perform euthanasia.

   Passive: _____

6. Protesters are going to intervene.

   Passive: _____

7. Religious groups will withhold support.

   Passive: _____

8. Legalizing euthanasia will jeopardize the government.

   Passive: _____

9. The government is going to hold a referendum.

   Passive: _____

10. Many people will sign a petition.

   Passive: _____

Exercise 7

■ Rewrite the sentences with modal auxiliaries below in the passive voice.

Reminder: To make an active sentence passive, the verb must take a direct object. Not all of the sentences can be rewritten.

1. Trevor and Troy can do the job tomorrow.
   Passive: *The job can be done tomorrow.*_____

2. Stacey and Caroline should supervise the work.

   Passive: _____

3. Daren could pick up the mail.

   Passive: _____

4. Carl can sweep the hall.

   Passive: _____

5. Her neighbour can water the plants.

Passive: _____

6. Her husband should clean up the mess.

Passive: _____

7. Her children could help out more.

Passive: _____

8. They must prepare the food.

Passive: _____

9. She should pay her bills.

Passive: _____

10. The substitute teacher may mark the essays.

Passive: _____

Exercise 8

▬ **Fill in the blanks with the correct form of the verb. Do not use contractions.**

The legalization of euthanasia (debate / present perfect) [1.] *has been debated* _____
in this country for a long time.

Proponents (argue / present perfect) [2.] _____ that
euthanasia ends pain and suffering.

Those opposed (counter / present perfect) [3.] _____ that
euthanasia is murder.

Which side (be / simple present) [4.] _____ right?

If I (be / simple past) [5.] _____ dying, I would want
the right to end my life. I (not think / simple present) [6.] _____
I would actually end my life—but I would like to have the option. Ironically,
knowing I could end the pain whenever I (want / simple past) [7.] _____
_____ would help me endure it.

In countries where euthanasia (legalize / present perfect) [8.] _____,
cases of abuse (occur / present perfect) [9.] _____. Such
cases (be / simple present) [10.] _____ unfortunate. Patients
(pressure / present perfect) [11.] _____ to end their lives:

hospitals (want / simple present) ^{12.} _____ to save money; children (hope / simple present) ^{13.} _____ to inherit their parents' money; and society (not want / simple present) ^{14.} _____ _____ to pay for futile treatments.

I (be / simple present) ^{15.} _____ aware that any law, including one legalizing euthanasia, can be abused. Laws (contravene / present continuous) ^{16.} _____ all the time! Nothing can be done to make sure that all laws (respected / simple present) ^{17.} _____ _____ all of the time.

The world in which we live (not be / simple present) ^{18.} _____ perfect. I guess the best we can do is hope that if euthanasia (legalize / simple present) ^{19.} _____ in Canada, any cases of abuse (keep / simple future) ^{20.} _____ to a minimum and prosecuted to the full extent of the law.

Exercise 9

- Write a 50- to 75-word paragraph about euthanasia. Begin your paragraph with: **The legalization of euthanasia has been debated in this country for a long time.**

- Provide a few reasons why the euthanasia question has not yet been settled. Use at least two verbs in the passive voice. Underline these two verbs.

Exercise 10

- Correct each of the sentences below.

1. A cheque is ~~send~~ once a month.

Correction(s): *sent* _____

2. The thief is being arrest.

Correction(s): _____

3. Was the money return?

Correction(s): _____

4. The jewellery has been returned?

Correction(s): _____

5. Lunch has not been serve.

Correction(s): _____

6. Will the assignment be submit on time?

Correction(s): _____

7. When the house was sold?

Correction(s): _____

8. Is the money going to be give away?

Correction(s): _____

9. Some help could to be offered.

Correction(s): _____

10. The test has been grade.

Correction(s): _____

Would You Like to Talk about It?

Activity 1: Passive Voice in Context

This is a paired conversation activity, which focuses on the passive voice in various tenses.

Required
• An English newspaper and a highlighter

Instructions
1. Read through an English newspaper with your partner, highlighting the first ten examples of the passive voice that you see.

2. Go back and re-read the passive voice examples in context.

3. Determine why the passive voice is being used in each example. Is the subject unknown? Unimportant? Is the *by* structure used to emphasize the performer of the action?

4. On a separate sheet of paper, write down the sentence in which the passive voice is used. Indicate the verb tense/form used. Rewrite the sentence in the active voice. If the subject is unknown, write "someone." For example:

The patient was given an overdose.
Tense: Simple past
Someone gave the patient an overdose.

5. As you complete this passive voice activity, feel free to discuss the current events in the newspaper.

Suggestion: Focus on newspaper headlines while doing this activity. You will often find abbreviated versions of the passive form in news headlines: Man Found Dead in Metro = A Man Was Found Dead in the Metro.

Activity 2: Trivia

This is a two-team activity designed to help you practise the passive voice in the simple past tense. For this activity, teams of two or three are best.

Required
• A sheet of lined paper, a pen or a pencil
• Research materials (optional)

Instructions

1. Each team writes five trivia questions about famous people and their accomplishments in the simple past using either the active or the passive voice. Each of the questions is then answered in the passive voice.

   For example:
   • Question 1: *Who was awarded the Academy Award for best actor in 2005?* (Answer: *Jamie Foxx **was awarded** the Academy Award for best actor in 2005.*)
   • Question 2: *Who cracked the DNA code?* (Answer: *The DNA code **was cracked** by James Watson and Francis Crick.*)
   • Question 3: *Who performed the world's first human heart transplant?* (Answer: *The world's first human heart transplant **was performed** by Professor Christiaan Barnard.*)
   • Question 4: *Who sculpted the statue of David?* (Answer: *The statue of David **was sculpted** by Michelangelo.*)
   • Question 5: *Who won the 2005 Tour de France?* (Answer: *The 2005 Tour de France **was won** by Lance Armstrong.*)

   Make sure the answers to all five questions are correct. You may need to do some research.

2. Team 1 asks Team 2 the first question. If Team 2 answers correctly, the members are awarded a point. If not, no point is awarded.
   Note: Team 2 must use the passive voice correctly in their response to get the point.

3. Team 2 asks Team 1 a question. If Team 1 answers correctly, the members are awarded a point. If not, no point is awarded.
   Note: Team 1 must use the passive voice correctly in their response to get the point.

4. Repeat steps two and three until all ten questions have been asked and answered.

5. The winner is the team that scores the most points.
   Note: If there is a tied score, go into a "lightning round": each team creates additional questions, and the first team to miss a question in a round loses the match.

Suggestion: Create questions based on what you are studying in your other courses. In this way, you can kill two birds with one stone: practise your English and review other subjects in your programme of study.

UNIT 9 | What's in a Name?

A noun is a word or a group of words that names people, places or things.

Names are extremely important: if you didn't have a name, who would you be?

In this unit, we won't consider philosophical questions as complex as the one just raised, but we will consider:

- kinds of nouns
- plural noun forms
- noncount nouns
- possessive nouns

What's in a name? A great deal, as you will soon see.

Did You Know?

Kinds of Nouns
There are four kinds of nouns:

1. **Common** (general)
   mother, father, baby ...

2. **Proper** (specific)
   Canada, Montreal, Rufus Wainwright ...

3. **Abstract** (things that are not concrete)
   love, hate, jealousy ...

4. **Collective** (group)
   team, group, herd ...

> **GRAMMAR TIP**
> Collective nouns take a singular verb when considered as a group or a plural verb when considered as individuals in a group.
>
> *The other team **is winning** the match.*
>
> *The other team **are wearing** blue and gold uniforms.*

Plural Noun Forms

Refer to the following chart for the rules concerning regular and irregular plurals.

Rules	Examples
Add "s" to the singular form of the noun.	mother ➡ mothers
Add "es" to nouns ending in "ch," "sh," "s," "x" or "o."	match ➡ matches bush ➡ bushes bus ➡ buses box ➡ boxes hero ➡ heroes
Nouns that end in "y": • Add "s" if a vowel precedes the "y." • Change the "y" to "i" and add "es" if a consonant precedes the "y."	boy ➡ boys baby ➡ babies
Most nouns ending in "f" or "fe": • Change the "f" or "fe" to "v" and add "es."	half ➡ halves self ➡ selves knife ➡ knives shelf ➡ shelves leaf ➡ leaves thief ➡ thieves life ➡ lives wife ➡ wives loaf ➡ loaves wolf ➡ wolves
Other nouns ending in "f" or "fe": • Add "s" to form the plural. Note: Some of these nouns have two plural forms.	reef ➡ reefs scarf ➡ scarfs scarf ➡ scarves
Some nouns form the plural by a vowel change.	fireman ➡ firemen mouse ➡ mice foot ➡ feet policeman ➡ policemen goose ➡ geese policewoman ➡ policewomen louse ➡ lice tooth ➡ teeth man ➡ men woman ➡ women
Some nouns have the same form in the singular and in the plural.	aircraft ➡ aircraft salmon ➡ salmon craft ➡ craft series ➡ series deer ➡ deer sheep ➡ sheep fish ➡ fish species ➡ species offspring ➡ offspring trout ➡ trout
Certain nouns are always plural.	clothes pliers police scissors pants goods pyjamas stairs eyeglasses surroundings
Words of Greek or Latin origin form their plurals according to the rules of those languages.	axis ➡ axes diagnosis ➡ diagnoses basis ➡ bases bacterium ➡ bacteria crisis ➡ crises emphasis ➡ emphases nucleus ➡ nuclei ovum ➡ ova hypothesis ➡ hypotheses datum ➡ data

Note: • Acronyms, decades, letters and numbers can be pluralized: RRSPs, 1980s, 7s.
- The usual plural of *person* is *people*, not *persons*.
- Words of foreign origin ending in "o" form their plural by adding "s" not "es":
  lasso ➡ ~~lassoes~~ lassos (from the Spanish word *lazo*.)
- Sometimes nouns that look plural are actually singular: AIDS, billiards, news.

> **PRONUNCIATION TIP**
>
> When a singular noun is pluralized by adding "s," the "s" can be pronounced in three different ways:
>
> 1. /z/ as in *mothers* for singular nouns ending in voiced sounds.
> 2. /s/ as in *pants* for singular nouns ending in voiceless sounds.
> 3. /iz/ as in *losses* for singular nouns ending in "s," "z," "sh," "ch," "x," "se," "ge" or "ce."

Noncount Nouns

Nouns that have a plural form are called count nouns.

Some nouns do not have a plural form: they are called noncount (or mass) nouns because they cannot be counted.

The following chart summarizes common noncount nouns:

Kinds of Noncount Nouns	Examples
No separate parts	coffee, meat, milk, soup, water
Parts too small to count	grass, hair, salt, sand, sugar
Refers to whole categories	clothing, food, furniture, homework, money
Abstract	advice, information, life, love, music
Academic subjects	chemistry, eugenics, history, mathematics, physics

Noncount nouns are not preceded by *a* or *an*. They may be preceded by:

- *some*
- *any*
- *much*
- *no*
- *a lot of*
- *a little of*
- *a piece of*
- *a cup of*
- *a bottle of*
- *a bowl of*

*They drank ~~a~~ **some coffee**.*
*Did she give you ~~an~~ **any advice**?*
*He does not have ~~a~~ **much clothing**.*

Noncount nouns always take a singular verb.
*My homework ~~are~~ **is** done.*

Use *there is* with noncount nouns and singular count nouns.
***There is** some mail.*
***There is** a letter.*

Use *there are* with plural count nouns.
***There are** two letters.*

> **GRAMMAR TIP**
>
> Use *many* with count nouns and *much* with noncount nouns.
>
> *They drank **many bottles** of wine.*
>
> *Do you have **much money**?*

Possessive Nouns

Nouns referring to people, places, animals and time can "possess":
Mr. Anderson's car, Montreal's stadium, the dogs' bones, Tuesday's class.

To indicate possession:

- Add *'s* to singular nouns and plural nouns not ending in "s":
  woman's work   people's lives

- Add an apostrophe only (') to plural nouns ending in "s":
  two boys' bikes

Would You Like to Practise?

Exercise 1

■ Indicate with a check mark whether each of the following nouns is common, proper, abstract or collective. The first one has been done for you.

If-Clauses	Common	Proper	Abstract	Collective
1. carrier	✔			
2. committee				
3. day				
4. disease				
5. doctor				
6. Down syndrome				
7. Dr. Jennings				
8. February				
9. gene				
10. health				
11. hospital				
12. life				
13. month				
14. Montreal General Hospital				
15. nurse				
16. pain				
17. suffering				
18. team				
19. test				
20. Tuesday				

Exercise 2

■ Pluralize each of the nouns in the chart below.

Singular	Plural	Singular	Plural
1. abnormality	*abnormalities*	11. process	
2. attorney		12. sandwich	
3. child		13. scan	
4. datum		14. shelf	
5. family		15. spokesman	
6. fetus		16. tax	
7. hero		17. tooth	
8. man		18. wish	
9. person		19. woman	
10. photo		20. thesis	

Exercise 3

■ Indicate whether the noun in italics is singular or plural.

Noun	Singular	Plural
1. Several *aircraft* have landed.		✔
2. An *aircraft* has crash-landed.		
3. He brought a *fish* for supper.		
4. *Fish* are plentiful in these waters.		
5. The *species* are endangered.		
6. The *species* is endangered.		
7. Have you read that *series* of books?		
8. That author is working on two new *series*.		
9. Her *offspring* are well raised.		
10. Her *offspring* is in jail.		

Exercise 4

■ Fill in the blanks using the correct form of the verb in parentheses.

1. Billiards (be / simple present) _____ *is* _____ a fascinating game.

2. His pyjamas (not hang / present continuous) _____
   on the clothesline.

3. Kevin's pants (be / simple present) _____ at the dry cleaner's.

4. Sadly, AIDS (devastate / present perfect) _____ much of sub-Saharan Africa.

5. Sally's clothes (lie / past continuous) _____ on the floor.

6. The coffee (taste / simple present) _____ good; I'll have another cup.

7. Steve's advice (be / simple past) _____ good.

8. The police (give / present perfect) _____ him a speeding ticket.

9. The surroundings (be / simple present) _____ rather depressing.

10. Fortunately, the news (be / simple present) _____ very good!

Exercise 5

■ **Indicate whether the following nouns are count or noncount.**

Hint: A noncount noun has no plural form.

Noun	Count	Noncount	Noun	Count	Noncount
1. air		✔	11. laughter		
2. blood			12. letter		
3. book			13. mail		
4. bread			14. mathematics		
5. corn			15. nature		
6. electricity			16. paper		
7. fun			17. peas		
8. gas			18. popcorn		
9. honesty			19. pork		
10. joke			20. sweater		

Exercise 6

■ **Underline the correct answer in parentheses.**

1. Would you like (a / a cup of) coffee?

2. (A / A piece of) furniture is being delivered tomorrow morning.

3. Her hair (is / are) dyed.

4. Their (homeworks are / homework is) due tomorrow.

5. The (information is / informations are) currently unavailable.

6. Pollution (endangers / endanger) one's health.

7. How about (a / some) yogourt?

8. How (much / many) wine did you buy?

9. How (much / many) bottles of wine do you want?

10. Mathematics (is / are) difficult.

Exercise 7

■ **Correct each sentence below, adding an apostrophe (') or an 's wherever necessary.**

1. Jane ultrasound is next week.

2. She is staying at her parents house until the baby comes; her mother and father are happy she is staying with them.

3. Jane is divorcing her husband, Gus; the couple divorce will be final next month.

4. Gus new girlfriend, Sheila, is not happy about the imminent birth.

5. Sheila already has three children; her children father died a few years ago.

6. Jane hopes next week ultrasound will go well.

7. The ultrasound will take place at Montreal Victoria Hospital.

8. While she is staying at her parents place, Jane best friend is taking care of her dogs.

9. Her dogs names are Brad and Pitt.

10. With Brad and Pitt in the house, Jane does not need Gus!

Exercise 8

■ **Read the passage and complete the chart that follows.**

Many disabled rights *activists* are concerned about genetic and prenatal testing and the resulting *prevention* and *elimination* of "abnormal" *fetuses*.

With genetic testing, *carriers* of genetic *illnesses* such as *Huntington*'s chorea and cystic *fibrosis* can choose not to have *children*. With amniocentesis, a diagnostic *procedure*, fetal *abnormalities* can be detected and the fetuses aborted.

It is no *secret* that *Canadians* welcome healthy and able-bodied children into *society* and spurn diseased and disabled *offspring*.

For activists, such a state of affairs is intolerable. In their *eyes* all *people*—able-bodied and disabled alike—have *value*, and society's *strength* is derived not from the elimination of genetic *diversity* but from the embracing of this diversity.

Noun	Kind			
	Common	**Proper**	**Abstract**	**Collective**
1. activists	✔			
2. prevention				
3. elimination			✔	
4. fetuses	✔			
5. carriers				
6. illnesses				
7. Huntington				
8. fibrosis				
9. children				
10. procedure				
11. abnormalities	✔			
12. secret			✔	
13. Canadians				
14. society				
15. offspring	✔			
16. eyes				
17. people	✔			
18. value			✔	
19. strength				
20. diversity			✔	

Exercise 9

■ Write a 50- to 75-word paragraph describing your classroom.

■ Begin your paragraph with: In this classroom, there is/are...

■ Describe one singular object (e.g., *There is a white ceiling.*) and four plural objects (e.g., *There are 25 desks.*).

■ Finally describe the atmosphere of the class using a noncount noun (e.g., *There is a lot of energy in the class.*).

Exercise 10

■ Correct each of the sentences below.

1. Several ~~bacterium~~ are present.
   Correction(s): *bacteria*

2. Can I give you an advice?
   Correction(s):

3. What are your hypothesis?
   Correction(s):

4. Where is David car?
   Correction(s):

5. That boys' bike is missing.
   Correction(s):

6. Three ovum must be extracted.
   Correction(s):

7. Mathematics are my favourite subject.
   Correction(s):

8. The datum are not available.
   Correction(s):

9. I have two homeworks due tomorrow.
   Correction(s):

10. She goes from one crises to the next.
    Correction(s):

Activity 1: Concepts in Your Life

In this activity, you will discuss some of life's most important subjects—and practise using noncount nouns!

Required
• a pen or a pencil

Instructions
1. With a partner, examine the chart below.
2. Discuss each abstract noun and arrive at a shared definition.
3. Fill in the chart.

Suggestion: For this activity, do not use a dictionary to look up definitions. Create your own definitions, based on your personal experience with these abstract concepts. Afterwards, it might be interesting to compare your definitions to those written by others in the class.

Abstract Noun	Definition
1. Beauty	*Beauty is...*
2. Courage	
3. Happiness	
4. Justice	
5. Laughter	
6. Love	

Abstract Noun	Definition
8. Peace	
9. Suffering	
10. Wealth	

Activity 2: Find Someone Who ...

This timed activity involves all class members. You will practise using count nouns—and get to know one another a little better.

Required
• A pen or a pencil

Instructions
1. Read through the Find Someone Who chart below.
2. Review yes/no question formation in the simple present tense for both *be* and other verbs (Unit 2).
3. When the teacher says "go," you have a maximum of five minutes to fill in the chart below with the names of ten of your classmates, one for each statement. Note: You must transform each statement into a question; for example, "Do you drink more than five cups of coffee a day?" (statement 1).
4. Whoever completes the chart first yells "done" and is declared the winner.
5. If no one is able to complete the chart, the winners are those who completed the chart the most.

Suggestion: Follow up this activity with a class discussion led by your teacher (or a class volunteer). For example, ask why the person drinks so much coffee (statement 1), how many years the person has exercised regularly (statement 2), etc.

Find Someone Who...	Person's Name
1. Drinks more than five cups of coffee a day.	
2. Exercises at least four times a week.	
3. Has a car.	
4. Is exactly 6 feet tall.	
5. Knows a famous person.	
6. Lives with five other people.	
7. Owns two pets.	
8. Spends more than three hours a day on the computer.	
9. Wears contact lenses.	
10. Weighs between 130 and 140 pounds.	

A pronoun is a word that stands for or replaces a noun. For example:

Sam *videotaped the recital.* ➡ **He** *videotaped the recital.*

Pronouns are important: without them, sentences would be repetitive and hard to understand.

Compare the following:
Kevin gave Susan a letter Kevin had written, and Susan read the letter.
*Kevin gave Susan a letter **he** had written, and **she** read it.*

In this unit, we will focus our attention on some of the more common types of pronouns.

Did You Know?

There are many different types of pronouns.

- **Personal**
  He *bought a new cell phone, but* **he** *does not know how to use* **it**.

- **Reflexive**
  She made **herself** *something to eat.*

- **Indefinite**
  Everybody *complained about the homework.*

- **Demonstrative**
  This *is my textbook.*

- **Possessive**
  Whose car did you take? We took **theirs**.

- **Relative**
  That is the person **who** *drove the car.*

Personal Pronouns

A personal pronoun may be singular or plural and act as a subject or object.

	Person	Subject	Object	Example
Singular	**first**	I	me	*I* told Todd to give *me* the keys.
	second	you	you	*You* were late even though the teacher had asked *you* to be on time.
	third	he/she/it	him/her/it	*She* gave *him* some money.
Plural	**first**	we	us	*We* insist that the money be given to *us*.
	second	you	you	*You* failed the exam, but the teacher will give each of *you* a make-up exam.
	third	they	them	*They* want the teacher to give *them* an extension.

Note: • *You* and *it* have the same subject and object forms.
　　　• Use *it* to refer to a thing or an animal.
　　　• Use *they* to refer to people, things or animals.

GRAMMAR TIP
~~Theirself, theirselves~~ and ~~hisself~~ do not exist in standard English.

Reflexive Pronouns

A reflexive pronoun refers back to the doer.

	Person	Subject	Example
Singular	**first**	myself	I gave *myself* a treat.
	second	yourself	You must behave *yourself*.
	third	himself/herself/itself	He asked *himself* if she loved him.
Plural	**first**	ourselves	We need to discipline *ourselves* to do our homework.
	second	yourselves	You should discipline *yourselves* to work harder.
	third	themselves	They invited *themselves* over for dinner.

Note: • The subject and the object are the same person.
　　　• The second person singular is *yourself*, and the second person plural is *yourselves*.
　　　• A reflexive pronoun can be used to emphasize a noun or a pronoun:
　　　　*Karen **herself** made the cake.*

Indefinite Pronouns

An indefinite pronoun does not refer to a specific person or thing. Some indefinite pronouns are singular, some plural and some are both.

Indefinite Pronoun	Singular	Plural	Indefinite Pronoun	Singular	Plural
1. anybody	X		12. someone	X	
2. anyone	X		13. one	X	
3. each	X		14. both		X
4. either	X		15. few		X
5. everybody	X		16. many		X
6. everyone	X		17. several		X
7. everything	X		18. all	X	X
8. neither	X		19. any	X	X
9. no one	X		20. none	X	X
10. nobody	X		21. most	X	X
11. somebody	X		22. some	X	X

Note: • In formal English, make sure your pronouns agree in number:
Everybody should do ~~their~~ her/his homework.
• For *none, some, any, most* and *all* use a singular verb if you want the subject to tell "how much," and use a plural verb if you want the subject to tell "how many."
***How much** of the room **was** painted? None was painted.*
***How many** of the rooms **were** painted? None were painted.*

Demonstrative Pronouns

Demonstrative pronouns point to a person or a thing, and they may be singular or plural.

	Near	Far	Example
Singular	this	that	*This is my shirt. That is yours.*
Plural	these	those	*These are my books. Those are yours.*

Note: • Typically, *this* and *these* refer to what is near and *that* and *those* to what is far.
• The pronouns *this, that, these* and *those* may also be used as adjectives:
***This shirt** is new. **Those shirts** are old.*

Possessive Pronouns

Possessive pronouns (and possessive adjectives) indicate ownership.

	Person	Possessive Adjective	Possessive Pronoun	Example
Singular	**first**	my	mine	Whose car is it? It's *my* car. It's *mine*.
	second	your	yours	Whose shirts are they? They're *your* shirts. They're *yours*.
	third	his/her/its	his/hers/its	Whose office is it? It's *her* office. It's *hers*.
Plural	**first**	our	ours	Whose books are they? They're *our* books. They're *ours*.
	second	your	yours	Whose classroom is it? It's *your* classroom. It's *yours*.
	third	their	theirs	Whose keys are they? They're *their* keys. They're *theirs*.

Note: • Do not confuse the contraction of "it is" (*it's*) with the possessive pronoun *its*.
• Do not confuse the contraction of "they are" (*they're*) with the possessive adjective *their* or the adverb *there*.
They're looking for *their* keys over *there*!

GRAMMAR TIP
See Appendix D for more information on dependent and independent clauses.

Relative Pronouns

Relative pronouns introduce relative clauses, dependent clauses that modify nouns and pronouns.

Use	Relative Pronoun			Example
	Subject	**Object**	**Possessive**	
People	who that	whom/who that	whose	There is the man *who* (or *that*) stole her purse. The man *whom* (or *who*, or *that*) I saw is over there. There is the woman *whose* purse was stolen.
Things	which that	which that	whose	That is the book *which* (or *that*) caused such uproar. Where is the book *which* (or *that*) I lent you? Here is the book *whose* cover is torn.

Note: • *Whom* is used primarily in formal English.
• In informal English, *that* may be used to refer to both people and things.
• When *who* and *that* are used as subjects, make sure that the verb that follows agrees with the noun or pronoun being modified:
Look at the men who ~~is~~ are standing over there.
Any book that ~~have~~ has a damaged cover must be returned.

Exercise 1

▬ **Replace the words in italics with the correct personal pronouns.**

1. It is *Susan* who was expelled from school. _____*she*_____

2. The teacher would like to see *you and your classmate*. _____

3. *The pies* are cooling on the windowsill. _____

4. Sally withdrew money and gave some to *Steve and me*. _____

5. Please put *the book* back on the shelf. _____

6. *My colleagues and I* would like a raise. _____

7. *The policeman* arrested the thief. _____

8. The community gave *the policeman* an award. _____

9. Give *Mrs. Anderson* the recipe. _____

10. Where did he install *the cameras*? _____

Exercise 2

▬ **Complete the sentences below with the correct reflexive pronouns.**

1. Jeff and Marilyn bought ___*themselves*___ a video camera.

2. Marilyn asked _____ whether they should videotape the new babysitter, Martha, with their young son.

3. Jeff told _____ that it was necessary.

4. Jeff _____ hooked up the video equipment.

5. The equipment _____ was easy to install.

6. The first day, Jeff and Marilyn caught the babysitter helping _____ to some money from Marilyn's purse.

7. Jeff and Marilyn questioned _____ about showing the tape to the police.

8. They decided to keep the tape to _____ and confront the babysitter.

9. The babysitter defended herself by saying, "Put _____ _____ in my shoes; if you only made seven dollars an hour, wouldn't you steal?"

10. Jeff and Marilyn replied, "No. Now put _____ in our shoes: We _____ hired you, and we _____ will fire you!"

Exercise 3

■ **Underline the correct word in parentheses. Use formal English.**

1. Some (<u>know</u> / knows) that hidden video cameras are everywhere.

2. Everybody should know that (their / his) actions are being recorded.

3. However, few (seem / seems) to be fully aware of this daily intrusion.

4. Whenever anyone (go / goes) into a corner store, (he is / they are) being taped.

5. Whenever anybody (buy / buys) gas, (his / their) licence plate is filmed.

6. If somebody (log / logs) on to (her / their) computer, a record is kept.

7. If someone (send / sends) an e-mail, a third party may read it.

8. If one (pay / pays) with a credit card, the transaction is filed.

9. No one (is / are) immune.

10. If anybody (think / thinks) that (he is / they are) immune, (he is / they are) kidding (himself / themselves)!

Exercise 4

▬ Underline the correct answer.

1. (<u>This</u> / That) is his car right here.

2. Take (these / those), not (these / those) over there.

3. (That / Those) was not the answer I was hoping for!

4. Where do I put (this / these)? Put it over there!

5. Where do I put (this / these)? Put them over there!

Exercise 5

▬ Replace the words in italics with the correct possessive pronouns.

1. That desk is *her desk*.   _____hers_____

2. Are those notebooks *their notebooks*?   _____

3. Is it *John's homework assignment*?   _____

4. That chair is *your chair*.   _____

5. That's *the dog's bone*.   _____

6. These pens are *my pens*.   _____

7. These sheets of paper are *Sue's sheets of paper*.   _____

8. This classroom is *our classroom*.   _____

9. Those pencils are *his pencils*.   _____

10. Your grade is the same as *my grade*.   _____

Exercise 6

▬ Fill in the blanks with the correct relative pronoun. Use formal English.

1. That is the car _____whose_____ tires need changing.

2. The house _____ is across the street is for sale.

3. The students _____ do the best often work the hardest.

4. The young mother _____ is rocking the baby looks tired.

5. The young woman with _____ you were speaking is my daughter.

6. There is the boy _____ mother passed away.

7. What is the meal _____ you like the most?

8. Where are the children _____ were playing in the park?

9. Where is the book _____ I borrowed from the library?

10. Where is the money _____ I gave you?

Exercise 7

■ **Underline the correct form of the verbs in parentheses.**

1. Most of the cameras that (was stolen / <u>were stolen</u>) (has been found / <u>have been found.</u>)

2. Most of the money that (was stolen / were stolen) (has been returned / have been returned) to the victim.

3. Several who (was arrested / were arrested) (has been freed / have been freed).

4. The little girls who (is playing / are playing) on the teeter-totter (is laughing / are laughing.)

5. The money that (is / are) on the table (belong / belongs) to my Uncle Frank.

6. The people who (is knocking / are knocking) at the front door (is / are) my neighbours.

7. The students in the back row who (was cheating / were cheating) (has been asked / have been asked) to leave the examination.

8. None of the students who (was caught / were caught) (has been suspended / have been suspended.)

9. The teacher who (was suspended / were suspended) (has been given / have been given) his job back.

10. The teachers who (was striking / were striking) (has agreed / have agreed) to negotiate.

Exercise 8

■ **Fill in the blanks with the pronouns in the list below:**

- anybody
- I
- myself
- which
- you
- he
- me
- that
- who
- yours
- him
- mine
- they
- whose
- yourself

Have you ever embarrassed ¹ ___*yourself*___ ? I have. Many times! Let ² _____ tell ³ _____ about it!

Usually, ⁴ _____ am a fairly discrete person ⁵ _____ minds his own business. Unfortunately one day, I let my curiosity get the better of me—and I snooped! I am ashamed to admit it, but there it is!

I have shared an office, ⁶ _____ has two desks, with my friend Bob for many years now. Bob is an older man ⁷ _____ refinement and generosity are admired by friends and colleagues alike. Indeed, ⁸ _____ is the epitome of good manners.

One day, I needed a pad to write down a phone message. I could not find a pad of my own, so I started rummaging around in Bob's desk. I came across a pad—and one of his pay stubs. Without thinking, I took out his pay stub to read it. As I was reading it, Bob walked into the office. When he noticed that I was reading his pay stub and not ⁹ _____ he simply said, "I believe ¹⁰ _____ is not ¹¹ _____ ." I could have kicked ¹² _____ in the pants. I apologized to ¹³ _____, of course, and he readily accepted my apology. However, our friendship has never been the same—and Bob now locks his desk drawers!

Well, ¹⁴ _____ say all things happen for a reason. If ¹⁵ _____ asked me what the reason for this embarrassing event was, I would say it was to teach me to curb my curiosity (or at least be more careful so as not to get caught!)

Exercise 9

■ Write a 50- to 75-word paragraph in which you describe a situation in which you snooped.

■ In your description, use at least four of the following six types of pronouns studied in this unit: personal, reflexive, indefinite, demonstrative, possessive and relative.

Exercise 10

▬ **Correct each of the sentences below.**

1. They bought ~~theirself~~ a good meal.

   Correction(s): *themselves*

2. Shauna and Sheila, you must discipline yourself to do better.

   Correction(s): _____

3. Most of the floor are washed.

   Correction(s): _____

4. Whose money is that? It's your.

   Correction(s): _____

5. This shirt over there is mine, and that shirt right here is his.

   Correction(s): _____

6. He went there hisself!

   Correction(s): _____

7. Where is it's bone?

   Correction(s): _____

8. Everybody must submit their assignment on time.

   Correction(s): _____

9. There is the boy which lost his mother.

   Correction(s): _____

10. We gave ourself a break.

    Correction(s): _____

Would You Like to Talk about It?

Activity 1: Proverbs

In this activity, you will work in pairs to practise various types of pronouns and examine ten English proverbs used for giving advice.

Required
• a pen or a pencil
• a dictionary

Instructions

1. With a partner, read through the ten proverbs below. Use a dictionary if necessary.
2. Working individually, each partner thinks of a problem he/she could share that would prompt the other partner to respond with one of the proverbs. For example:

   Problem: Applying to university is such a long process. There are booklets to read, recommendation letters to get and dozens of forms to fill out. It's all too much for me!
   Response: *Well, if you want something, you must work for it! Remember, the sooner you get started, the sooner you will finish.*

3. Partner A recounts his/her problem to Partner B, and Partner B selects one proverb from the list and responds to Partner A's problem.
4. Partner B recounts his/her problem to Partner A, and Partner A selects one proverb from the list and responds to Partner B's problem.
5. Repeat steps 2–4 until all the proverbs have been used. Note: Don't target the same proverb twice; try to use all ten proverbs.

Proverb List

- If you want something, you must work for it.
- He who hesitates is lost.
- It is no use crying over spilt milk.
- It takes two to tango.
- Nothing ventured, nothing gained.
- Scratch my back, and I will scratch yours.
- What you don't know, can't hurt you.
- You can't win them all.
- You cannot have your cake and eat it too.
- You cannot judge a book by its cover!

Suggestion: It's more interesting to use real rather than imaginary problems. As much as possible, base your problems on real-life situations.

Activity 2: Talking about Nouns

This activity works best in groups of four to six. It is designed to help you practise nouns and pronouns.

Required

- Four slips of paper for each member of the group
- A pen or a pencil
- A hat or small container

Instructions

1. Each group member writes down one common noun, one proper noun, one collective noun and one abstract noun—each on a separate slip of paper. (See page 94 for examples of these nouns.)
   Note: Members do not show one another what they have written.
2. All the slips of paper are placed in a hat (or small container).
3. The member whose last name is closest to the letter "z" begins. He/She selects a slip of paper and shows it to the person seated on his/her left.

4. The two members begin talking about the noun **indirectly**, only referring to the noun with pronouns. Take the abstract noun "love" for example. An indirect conversation would sound something like this:

*Do you know what **this** is?*
*No, I've never experienced **it** myself.*
*Some people say **it** is the best thing in life.*
*Well, I know that people fall in and out of **it** all the time …*

5. As other group members think they know what the two are talking about, they join in the conversation. The conversation continues until everyone is **obviously** talking about the same thing.

6. Continue in a clockwise manner, with the person who selects a slip of paper always showing it to the person seated on his/her left.

7. The activity ends when all the slips of paper have been selected.

Suggestion: Repeat the activity, this time focusing on only one type of noun: common, proper, collective or abstract.

Could You Describe That?

Adjectives describe nouns or pronouns.
*Vicki has a **new** car; it is **blue**.*

Adverbs describe verbs, adjectives or other adverbs.
*Vicki drives her **brilliantly** blue car **fairly quickly**.*

There are many different types of adjectives and adverbs, many of which you have already seen in this textbook.

In this unit, we will focus our attention on two of the more common types:
• adjectives of quality, and
• adverbs of manner.

Did You **Know**?

Adjectives of Quality

Adjectives of quality indicate "which kind" of noun or pronoun and may be divided into two broad categories:

1. **Opinion**
   nice, intelligent, beautiful, horrible, delicious, etc.

2. **Fact**
   big, new, flat, orange, Canadian, etc.

A fact adjective precedes the noun it modifies:
*He bought a **new** car.*

Opinion adjectives precede fact adjectives:
*He married ~~a Canadian intelligent~~ an **intelligent Canadian** doctor.*

> **GRAMMAR TIP**
> Adjectives of quality do not agree in number with the nouns they modify:
> *~~plastics~~ plastic chairs.*

Simple, Comparative and Superlative Adjective Forms

Most adjectives of quality have three forms: simple, comparative and superlative.

	Simple	Comparative	Superlative
One-syllable adjectives	short	shorter (than)	(the) shortest
Two-syllable adjectives ending in "y"	heavy	heavier (than)	(the) heaviest
Other two-syllable adjectives	splendid	more splendid (than)	(the) most splendid
Three-or-more-syllable adjectives	elegant	more elegant (than)	(the) most elegant
Common irregular adjectives	good bad little a lot	better (than) worse (than) less (than) more (than)	(the) best (the) worst (the) least (the) most

Note: • The comparative form is used to compare two people or things:
Jane is *shorter than* Alexandra.
• The superlative form is used to compare three or more people or things:
Jane is 120 pounds; Alexandra is 130 pounds; and Isabella is 135 pounds. Of the three, Isabella is *the heaviest.*
• The following one-syllable adjectives use the *more* and *most* forms: bored and tired.
For example: *more tired* and *most tired.*
• The following two-syllable adjectives use both the "er" and "est" forms as well as the *more* and *most* forms:
simple, common, handsome, quiet, gentle, narrow, clever, friendly and angry.
For example: *handsomer* or *more handsome* and *handsomest* or *most handsome.*

GRAMMAR TIP
Only adjectives of quality that are **not absolute** can be used in the comparative or the superlative forms:

Mary's essay was ~~more perfect~~ *better than Steve's.*

SPELLING TIP
• One-syllable adjectives ending in a "consonant + vowel + consonant" double the last consonant before adding "er" or "est": *hot* ➡ *hotter* ➡ *hottest.*
• One-syllable adjectives ending in "e" simply add "r" or "st": *blue* ➡ *bluer* ➡ *bluest.*
• Two-syllable adjectives ending in a consonant + "y" change the "y" to "i" before adding "er" or "est": *pretty* ➡ *prettiest.*

Special Case: Articles "A" and "An"

The indefinite articles *a* and *an* are both indefinite articles and adjectives.

A is used before words beginning with a "consonant sound": *a boy, a table, a university.*
Note: *University* begins with a consonant sound even though the first letter is a vowel.

An is used before words beginning with a "vowel sound": *an apple, an orange, an hour.*

Note: *Hour* begins with a vowel sound even though the first letter is a consonant.

Adverbs of Manner

Adverbs of manner indicate how something happens. Many adverbs of manner are formed by adding "ly" to the corresponding adjectives:

nice ➡ ***nicely***
intelligent ➡ ***intelligently***
enormous ➡ ***enormously***

Some adjectives of quality and adverbs of manner have the same form: *hard, fast* and *kindly*.

Adverb Position

Generally, the adverb of manner goes after the verb:
*He drove **quickly**.*

If there is an object, the adverb of manner goes after the object:
*He drove his car **quickly**.*

However if the object is long, the adverb of manner goes before the verb:
*He **quickly** drove the new car that he bought a week ago last Friday.*

GRAMMAR TIP
Never place an adverb between the verb and the object:
He drove ~~quickly~~ his car.

Simple, Comparative and Superlative Adverb Forms

Most adverbs of manner have three forms: simple, comparative and superlative.

	Simple	**Comparative**	**Superlative**
One-syllable adverbs	fast	faster (than)	(the) fastest
Two-syllable adjectives ending in "y"	bravely	more bravely (than)	(the) most bravely
Common irregular adverbs	well badly	better (than) worse (than)	(the) best (the) worst

SPELLING TIP
• If the adjective ends in a consonant + "y," change the final "y" to an "i" before adding "ly": *merry* ➡ ***merrily***.
• If the adjective ends in a consonant + "le," drop the "e" before adding "y": *ample* ➡ ***amply***.
• If the adjective ends in "ic," add "ally": *basic* ➡ ***basically***.
• The adjectives *true, due* and *whole* drop the final "e" before adding "ly": *true* ➡ ***truly***; *due* ➡ ***duly***; *whole* ➡ ***wholly***.

GRAMMAR TIP
Use the structure "as...as" with adjectives and adverbs to make comparisons of equality:
*His son is **as tall as** he is.*
*His mother drives **as quickly as** he does.*

Exercise 1

▬ Indicate whether each of the following adjectives of quality is an opinion or a fact adjective. The first one has been done for you.

Adjective	Opinion	Fact	Adjective	Opinion	Fact
1. American		✔	11. elegant		
2. beautiful			12. expensive		
3. big			13. luxurious		
4. black			14. new		
5. blue			15. South American		
6. Canadian			16. tacky		
7. chemical			17. terrific		
8. competent			18. ugly		
9. courageous			19. Victorian		
10. dangerous			20. young		

Exercise 2

▬ Underline the correct answer. Remember: Opinion adjectives precede fact adjectives.

1. Carl and Adam live in a (<u>luxurious Victorian</u> / Victorian luxurious) mansion.

2. Has he talked to you about his (new terrific / terrific new) job?

3. He bought an (expensive American / American expensive) car.

4. Kerry rented a (big beautiful / beautiful big) villa for the holidays.

5. Mary works for (a South American elegant / an elegant South American) woman.

6. They removed some (dangerous chemical / chemical dangerous) insulation from the attic.

7. She wore (an ugly black / a black ugly) dress to the dinner.

8. The other team is wearing (tacky blue / blue tacky) uniforms.

9. She is a (Canadian competent / competent Canadian) doctor.

10. She is a (courageous young / young courageous) woman.

Exercise 3

■ Rewrite each adjective in its comparative and superlative forms. Sometimes, more than one form is possible. Watch the spelling!

Simple	Comparative	Superlative	Simple	Comparative	Superlative
1. angry	*angrier* *more angry*	*angriest* *most angry*	11. hot		
2. big			12. lazy		
3. clever			13. nice		
4. easy			14. red		
5. fine			15. sad		
6. friendly			16. simple		
7. funny			17. steady		
8. gentle			18. thin		
9. happy			19. white		
10. heavy			20. wide		

Exercise 4

■ Write the comparative or superlative forms of the adjectives in parentheses.

1. After initiating drug therapy, patients often feel (bad) _____worse_____ than they did before; after a couple of weeks, they generally feel (good) _____better_____ than before.

2. He can honestly say that, right now, he is feeling (bad) _____ than he has ever felt in his life.

3. Of the many drugs she has tried, this was (good) _____.

4. Patented prescription drugs are (expensive) _____ today than ten years ago.

5. Pharmaceutical companies are (profitable) _____ than in the past.

6. She is (skinny) _____ now than when she first started therapy.

7. Since the company was awarded the patent, it has had a (big) _____ _____ share of the market.

8. The biopharmaceutical companies have developed (simple) _____ _____ tests.

9. The new drug is certainly (fast) _____ treatment on the market.

10. Their (new) _____ patent has given them (big) _____ share of the cancer drug market.

Exercise 5

■ Indicate whether the following terms are preceded by *a* or *an*.

Terms	A	An	Terms	A	An
1. patent	✔		11. breakthrough		
2. society			12. UNESCO declaration		
3. inventor			13. ethical problem		
4. hand			14. US patent		
5. invention			15. university		
6. bacterium			16. era		
7. gene			17. award		
8. AIDS cocktail			18. American college		
9. income			19. 18-hour experiment		
10. autoimmune disease			20. hoopla		

Exercise 6

■ Rewrite each of the following adjectives as adverbs.

Adjective	Adverb	Adjective	Adverb
1. happy	*happily*	11. basic	
2. scientific		12. angry	
3. generous		13. true	
4. loud		14. gentle	
5. careful		15. greedy	
6. lucky		16. ironic	
7. due		17. whole	
8. hard		18. easy	
9. good		19. quick	
10. bad		20. fast	

Exercise 7

■ **Circle the correct answer.**

1. Charlie was going through his medication _____ he should have.
   (a) more fast than
   (b) faster than ⊙

2. Of all the people I have ever known, she approached her illness _____.
   (a) the most brave
   (b) the most bravely
   (c) more bravely

3. She approached her illness _____ anybody else I have ever known.
   (a) bravely than
   (b) more bravely than
   (c) the most bravely than

4. Children respond _____ to drug treatments than the middle-aged or elderly.
   (a) more positively
   (b) most positively

5. Unfortunately, Kieran responded to the drug _____ he should have.
   (a) badly
   (b) worse than
   (c) the worst than

6. Of the three researchers, Dr. Stevens worked _____.
   (a) well
   (b) better
   (c) best

7. Which of the following is correct?
   (a) They applied quickly for a patent.
   (b) They applied for a patent quickly.

8. She _____ from her procedure.
   (a) awakened groggily
   (b) groggily awakened

9. Which of the following is correct?

   (a) They applied for the patent that would make them rich happily.

   (b) They happily applied for the patent that would make them rich.

10. Which of the following is correct?

   (a) They vigorously denied accusations of human gene patent infringement.

   (b) They denied vigorously accusations of human gene patent infringement.

   (c) They denied accusations of human gene patent infringement vigorously.

Exercise 8

■ **Fill in the blanks with the adjectives and adverbs in the list below:**

• antiretroviral	• healthier	• strict
• better	• increased	• the most promising
• completely	• more serious	• truly
• consistently	• new	• undetectable
• faithfully	• quickly	• well

I must say that I am __*truly*__ [1.] impressed with all the advances that have been made in HIV treatment.

With _____ [2.] and improved _____ [3.] medication, people infected with HIV are living longer and _____ [4.] lives.

Unfortunately, some people think that AIDS, the syndrome caused by HIV, has been cured; however, nothing could be further from the truth. While some people _____ [5.] respond to treatment, others do not respond at all. For those who do respond _____ [6.], many have unpleasant side effects: diarrhea, headache and nausea are common. Other _____ [7.] side effects can also occur: liver damage, anaemia and kidney stones.

Another difficulty with antiretroviral medication is the _____ [8.] regimen that patients must follow: if patients do not _____ [9.] take their antiretroviral medication, they run an _____ [10.] risk of developing drug resistance. Even if HIV becomes _____ [11.] in a patient, this does not mean that the patient has been _____ [12.] cured. Patients must _____ [13.] take their medication for life because HIV can hide in lymph nodes and the nervous system.

While those with HIV have a _____ [14.] prognosis today than ten or twenty years ago, HIV remains a serious disease, and _____ [15.] cure for AIDS is still the prevention of HIV transmission.

GRAMMAR TIP
Get, meaning *become*, is often followed by an adjective in various expressions: *get hungry, get tired, get even, get married, get divorced*, etc.

Exercise 9

▬ Write a 50- to 75-word paragraph in which you describe yourself and how you live your life. Use three adjectives to describe your physical appearance and two adjectives to describe your personality. Use a minimum of two adverbs to describe the way you live.

Exercise 10

▬ Correct each of the sentences below.

1. I ~~truely~~ don't believe a word she says!

   Correction(s): *truly* _____

2. He is a young handsome man.

   Correction(s): _____

3. She is wearing a pink gaudy sweatshirt.

   Correction(s): _____

4. She is an American amusing columnist.

   Correction(s): _____

5. He doesn't have a original idea in his head!

   Correction(s): _____

6. They visited an European old village.

   Correction(s): _____

7. She is more good than he is.

   Correction(s): _____

8. Today is hoter than yesterday.

   Correction(s): _____

9. She ate as fastly as he did.

   Correction(s): _____

10. Scientificly speaking, that doesn't make sense.

    Correction(s): _____

Activity 1: Your Likes

In this activity, you will practise using adjectives and adverbs in the comparative and superlative forms.

Required
- Questionnaire (below)
- A dictionary

Instructions
1. Read through the questionnaire.
2. Partner A begins, asking Partner B one "Which do you like more..." question followed by one "Which do you like most..." question.
3. Partner B answers the questions, explaining his/her choices.

   For example:
   Partner A: *Which do you like more? Cats or dogs?*
   Partner B: *I like dogs more. Dogs are smarter and more fun to be with. They interact better with people.* Etc.
   Partner A: *Which do you like most? Reading newspapers, magazines or books?*
   Partner B: *I like reading magazines best. Magazines are faster to read than books and have more pictures than newspapers.* Etc.

4. Partner B continues, asking Partner A one "Which do you like more..." question followed by one "Which do you like most..." question.
5. Partner A answers the questions, explaining his/her choices.
6. Repeat steps 2–5 until all the questions have been asked and answered.

Suggestion: Exchange questions and repeat the activity—or make up similar questions of your own.

Questionnaire

Partner A
Which do you like more?
1. Cats or dogs.
2. Eating out or eating in.
3. Going to a movie or renting a DVD.
4. Saving money or spending money.
5. Spending time with children or spending time with adults.

Which do you like most?

6. Reading newspapers, magazines or books.
7. Surfing the Internet, watching TV or doing crafts.
8. Taking the bus, driving in heavy traffic or travelling by subway.
9. Vacationing at the beach, in the mountains or at a lake.
10. Watching dramas, comedies or action-adventure films.

Partner B
Which do you like more?

1. Studying or working.
2. Summer or winter.
3. Taking a photograph or being photographed.
4. Walking in the country or walking in the city.
5. Working alone or working in a group.

Which do you like most?

6. Eating Italian, Mexican or Thai food.
7. English, philosophy or physical education.
8. Mowing the lawn, washing the car or weeding the garden.
9. Pop music, rap or classical.
10. Reading a book, working out at the gym or playing video games.

Activity 2: Famous People

This activity works best in teams of three or four. It is designed to help you practise adjectives.

Required
• A few sheets of paper
• A pen or a pencil
• Some research materials

Instructions
1. Each team brainstorms the names of five famous living people.
2. Team members write five increasingly specific descriptive sentences about each famous person. For example:

Céline Dion
1. *She is a Quebecker.* (general)
2. *She is a singer.*
3. *Her music is best described as "contemporary pop."*
4. *She has one child, a son.*
5. *She sang the theme song of the movie* The Titanic.
Try to use as many adjectives as possible in each descriptive sentence.

3. Team 1 selects one famous person and reads the first descriptive sentence to Team 2. If Team 2 guesses the identity of the famous person, Team 2 wins five points. If not, another clue is read. If Team 2 guesses after the second clue, Team 2 wins four points. If Team 2 guesses after the third clue, Team 2 wins three points, and so on. If Team 2 does not guess the identity of the famous person after all five descriptive sentences have been read, Team 1 wins five points.

4. Team 2 selects one famous person and reads the first descriptive sentence to Team 1. If Team 1 guesses the identity of the famous person, Team 1 wins five points. If not, another clue is read. If Team 1 guesses after the second clue, Team 1 wins four points. If Team 1 guesses after the third clue, Team 1 wins three points, and so on. If Team 1 does not guess the identity of the famous person after all five descriptive sentences have been read, Team 2 wins five points.

5. Repeat steps 3 and 4 until both teams have described all five famous people.

6. The winning team is the team with the most points at the end of the game.

Suggestion: Repeat the activity, this time using famous deceased people; in this way, you will also get a chance to practise the past tenses.

Common Information Question Words

Information Question Words	Examples
Who	*Who* did Bob marry? Bob married *Elizabeth*. *Who* saw Bob at the wedding? *Bob's family* saw him.
What	*What* do you want for supper? I want *pizza*. *What* was happening out there? *Two men were fighting*.
Where	*Where* do they live? They live in *Montreal*.
When	*When* do you leave for Europe? We leave *at the end of the month*.
Why	*Why* do you work so hard? Because I *want to get good marks*.
Whose	*Whose* car is that? That's *Jane's* car.
Which	*Which* shirt will you buy? I will buy the *brown shirt*, not the green shirt.
How	*How* does she get such good marks? She *studies every day*.
How far	*How far* is Montreal from Toronto? It's about *600 km*.
How much/many	*How much* money do you have with you? I have about *20 dollars*. *How many* books did he buy? He bought *11 books*.
How long	*How long* is today's class? It's about *three hours*.
How often	*How often* do you go to the supermarket? About *once a week*.

Note: • **Who and *what* can be used as subjects or objects.**
  Who did you see? (Object)   *Who* saw you? (Subject)
  What do you want? (Object)   *What* is that? (Subject)
 • ***Whom* is used as an object in formal English.**
  Whom did you see?
 • ***How much* is used with uncountable nouns and *how many* is used with countable nouns.**
  How much coffee is left? (Coffee, a liquid, is uncountable.)
  How many cups of coffee have you had today? (Cups are countable.)

APPENDIX B — Common Irregular Verbs

The verb chart below lists 100 common irregular verbs.

Base Form	Simple Past	Past Participle	Base Form	Simple Past	Past Participle
be	was, were	been	fall	fell	fallen
become	became	become	feed	fed	fed
begin	began	begun	feel	felt	felt
bend	bent	bent	fight	fought	fought
bet	bet	bet	find	found	found
bite	bit	bitten	fit	fit	fit
bleed	bled	bled	fly	flew	flown
blow	blew	blown	forbid	forbade	forbidden
break	broke	broken	forget	forgot	forgotten
bring	brought	brought	forgive	forgave	forgiven
build	built	built	freeze	froze	frozen
burst	burst	burst	get	got	gotten
buy	bought	bought	give	gave	given
catch	caught	caught	go	went	gone
choose	chose	chosen	grow	grew	grown
come	came	come	hang	hung	hung
cost	cost	cost	have	had	had
cut	cut	cut	hear	heard	heard
deal	dealt	dealt	hide	hid	hidden
dig	dug	dug	hit	hit	hit
do	did	done	hold	held	held
draw	drew	drawn	hurt	hurt	hurt
drink	drank	drunk	keep	kept	kept
drive	drove	driven	know	knew	known
eat	ate	eaten	lay	laid	laid

Base Form	Simple Past	Past Participle	Base Form	Simple Past	Past Participle
lead	led	led	show	showed	shown
leave	left	left	shut	shut	shut
lend	lent	lent	sing	sang	sung
let	let	let	sit	sat	sat
lie	lay	lain	sleep	slept	slept
light	lit	lit	slide	slid	slid
lose	lost	lost	speak	spoke	spoken
make	made	made	spend	spent	spent
mean	meant	meant	stand	stood	stood
meet	met	met	steal	stole	stolen
pay	paid	paid	swim	swam	swum
put	put	put	swing	swung	swung
quit	quit	quit	take	took	taken
read	read	read	teach	taught	taught
ride	rode	ridden	tear	tore	torn
ring	rang	rung	tell	told	told
rise	rose	risen	think	thought	thought
run	ran	run	throw	threw	thrown
say	said	said	understand	understood	understood
see	saw	seen	wake	woke	woken
seek	sought	sought	wear	wore	worn
sell	sold	sold	win	won	won
send	sent	sent	wind	wound	wound
shake	shook	shaken	withdraw	withdrew	withdrawn
shoot	shot	shot	write	wrote	written

Common Regular Verbs

The verb chart below lists 100 common regular verbs in the simple past tense. Verbs are classified according to the pronunciation of the final "ed" ending.

/t/	/d/	/id/
announced	agreed	accepted
asked	allowed	admitted
attached	answered	appreciated
attacked	approved	attempted
baked	argued	attracted
balanced	banned	avoided
booked	bathed	cheated
clapped	called	collected
confessed	carried	communicated
danced	caused	competed
developed	changed	concentrated
disliked	claimed	consisted
dressed	cleaned	decided
dropped	closed	depended
fixed	compared	detected
increased	complained	divided
influenced	considered	educated
introduced	described	injected
jumped	disagreed	intended
kissed	disapproved	interested
knocked	earned	invented
packed	failed	interrupted
passed	gathered	irritated
picked	identified	landed
placed	informed	lasted
possessed	jogged	objected
practised	killed	painted
smoked	married	permitted
talked	moved	pointed
thanked	offered	presented
touched	planned	recorded
washed	stayed	started
wiped	warned	visited
worked		

Punctuation

Punctuation	Use	Examples
Periods	After sentences	It is wrong.
	With abbreviations	It is 9:00 a.m.
Question Marks	After direct questions	Did you do your homework?
	After question tags	You did your homework, didn't you?
Exclamation Marks	To express strong emotion	She won the lottery!
Commas	Between independent clauses joined by a coordinate conjunction	Sue went on vacation, and she had a great time.
	In a series	She went dancing, surfing, shopping and scuba diving.
	Between coordinate adjectives	Kevin wore a grey, green and blue tie.
	After introductory words	Unfortunately, she didn't get the job.
	After introductory phrases	To get good marks, students must study.
	After introductory clauses	When she studies, she does well.
	Before direct quotations	As the saying goes, "All is fair in love and war."
	Between two consecutive numbers	In 2004, 3500 Canadians were waiting for an organ donation.
Semicolons	Between independent clauses	Jane passed; her friend Kelly failed.
Colons	Before a list	She asked me to buy the following items: eggs, milk and bread.
	After "note"	Note: Applications must be received by March 15.
	Between hours and minutes	It's 2:15 p.m.
Quotation Marks	For direct quotations	"Excuse me," he said, "I didn't understand."
	For titles of works contained in another work (articles, book chapters, TV episodes, etc.)	Did you read the article, "Cloning Becomes Freakshow"?
Underscores	For titles of complete works (newspapers, magazines, books, TV series, movies, etc.)	Did your teacher use <u>Parallels: Taking a Stand in English</u>?
Apostrophes	With contractions	I don't think he'll be here.
	With possessive nouns	Where is Bob's house?
Parentheses	With references to pages, units, appendices, etc.	Review the simple present and present continuous tenses (Unit 1).

Note: • Do not use periods with abbreviations that are in capital letters: HIV, AIDS, RRSP, etc.
  • Coordinate conjunctions include: *for, and, nor, but, or, yet, so.*
  • Don't use a comma after *hence, thus, then* or *still* when used as introductory words: Then he did his homework.
  • For quotations within quotations, use both double and single quotation marks: Kerry replied, "My friend said, 'I'll be back in two hours.'"
  • When using a word processor, italics may be used instead of underscores to indicate titles of complete works: Did your teacher use *Parallels: Taking a Stand in English*?

Capitalization

Use for	Examples
The first word of a sentence	*Her* course is interesting.
The first person singular	Where should *I* go?
Direct quotations of complete sentences	Her lawyer said, *"You* will win your case."
The first word of each item in a list	Do not forget to bring the following items to your final exam: (1) *Textbook* (2) *Class* notes (3) *Graded* compositions.
Courtesy and job titles, first and family names	*Mr.* and *Mrs. Anderson, Mayor Adams* and his companion *Ms. Anita Brown* are here to see you.
All important words in a title	The local bookstore sold more than 500 copies of *Harry Potter and the Philosopher's Stone.* I bought two copies: one for me and one for my friend.
Weekdays, months, holidays	Today is *Saturday, December* 24. Tomorrow is *Christmas.*
Countries, languages, nationalities, races and religions	In three days, I am leaving for *Cuba* where the people speak *Spanish.* Many *Cubans* are *Christians* or *Santerians.* The *Santeria* religion was introduced to *Cuba* by *African* slaves.
Specific place names	I live on *Greene Avenue* in *Montreal.*
Acronyms	She has been living with ~~human immunodeficiency virus~~ *HIV* for many years.

Note: • Capitalize all words in a title except articles and conjunctions or prepositions *unless* the article, conjunction or preposition is the first or last word in a title or follows a period, colon or a dash.
> *An English Grammar: A New Approach for Students of English as a Second Language.*
• Unlike the courtesy title *Mrs., Ms.* makes no referral to marital status.

Common Verbs Followed by Gerunds or Infinitives

A gerund is the "ing" form of a verb: *eat* ➡ ***eating***. An infinitive is the simple form of the verb preceded by the preposition *to*: *eat* ➡ ***to eat***. When two verbs are used together, the second verb is either a gerund or an infinitive:

The thief admitted ~~to steal~~ stealing the money.
She agreed ~~selling~~ to sell her car.
He likes to eat pizza. He likes eating pizza.

Modal verbs are an exception to this rule, as they are immediately followed by the simple form of the verb:

The teacher might ~~to let~~ let us leave early.

To know which form to use, you can refer to lists like the one below, or you can look the first verb up in a dictionary for an example of correct usage.

Verbs Followed by Gerunds		Verbs Followed by Infinitives	
admit	mention	agree	manage
advise	mind	appear	mean
anticipate	miss	arrange	need
appreciate	practise	ask	offer
avoid	quit	claim	plan
complete	recommend	decide	prepare
consider	regret	demand	pretend
deny	resent	deserve	promise
discuss	resist	expect	refuse
enjoy	risk	fail	seem
finish	suggest	hope	wait
forget	understand	intend	want
keep		learn	

NOTES